THE
FRONT
ROW
FACTOR

JON VROMAN

Foreword by **Hal Elrod**

THE FRONT ROW FACTOR

TRANSFORM YOUR LIFE *with* **THE ART OF MOMENT MAKING**

Published by Front Row Global

Copyright 2017 © Jon Vroman

ASIN: B01N4VO1WG

Print ISBN: 978-1544037592

Interior Design: Christina Culbertson, 3CsBooks.com

A portion of all royalties from The Front Row Factor are donated to the Front Row Foundation.

By purchasing this book, you are helping someone who is facing a life-threatening illness have a front row experience at the live event of their dreams.

Thank you for being a moment maker.

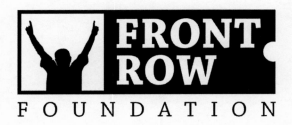

Dedicated to

Tatyana

Tiger

&

Ocean

You make each moment count.

YOU'RE INVITED

The world is so empty if one thinks only of mountains, rivers & cities; but to know someone who thinks and feels with us, and who, though distant, is close to us in spirit, this makes the earth for us an inhabited garden.

— Johann Wolfgang von Goethe

WE'VE CREATED A PLACE FOR YOU, THE MOMENT makers of the world, to connect, collaborate, create, and celebrate together. You are invited to join our online community, or as we say—our Front Row Family.

Visit FrontRowFactor.com/facebook and request to join a group of happy, creative, and generous people from around the world who choose to make the most of every moment by living life in the front row. I'll be there personally and I look forward to seeing you there.

At the end of this book, you'll hear about The Front Row Moment Experiment. Trust me, you'll love it. Make sure to check out the free resources we created just for you at FrontRowFactor.com/experiment.

To connect with me on social media, you'll find me on Twitter and Instagram at @jonvroman and on Facebook at Facebook.com/jonvroman. Get access to the Front Row Factor podcast and all other resources at FrontRowFactor.com.

TABLE OF CONTENTS

Foreword by Hal Elrod v

Opening Act:
Make the Most of Every Moment ix

PART I:
A Front Row Life

Chapter 1: A Deeper Meaning 1

Invest in yourself and others.

Chapter 2: Life *Is* Different in the Front Row 7

You might not choose your seat, but you can always
choose a front row experience.

Chapter 3: Ultra-Purpose 13

When your *why* has heart, your *how* gets legs.

Chapter 4: Front Row Foundation 21

Learning about life from those fighting for it.

PART II:
Compelling Forces

Chapter 5: Hope for the Future 37

What makes you come alive?

Chapter 6: Celebrate Our Experiences 55

What are your "front row" moments?

Chapter 7: Live in the Moment 71

Amplify the good, silence what's not.

Part III:
Front Row Focus

Chapter 8: Cultivate an Empowering Mindset 87

What's in your control?

Chapter 9: Cultivate Empowering Relationships 113

Who will you stand for?

Chapter 10: Cultivate Empowering Environments 137

How will you create an environment that helps you come alive?

Part IV:
The Front Row Movement

Chapter 11: Building Momentum 163

How can moment making be your new rhythm?

Encore: Being A Moment Maker 175

The Front Row Family—*It's a Forever Thing*

The Front Row Moment Experiment 191

How can you be a daily moment maker and inspire others?

P.S. Special Note to You, The Moment Maker 211

Endnotes 214

A Personal Invitation 217

Acknowledgements 219

The Front Row Pose 233

About the Author 235

FOREWORD

by Hal Elrod

DO YOU LIVE LIFE IN THE FRONT ROW? **Or** do you allow the difficult circumstances you encounter to determine how you feel and how you live your life? In today's world, it is so easy to get carried away by all the activities that fill our days. Life moves so fast, sometimes at a pace too quick for us to notice.

Amid all this hustle and bustle, Jon Vroman found he did not want life to pass him by, but wanted to make every moment count. He was driven to create a framework to help us enjoy every single moment—even the challenging ones. This came from his understanding that we have a choice: We can choose to make the most of our lives, or we can let our circumstances dictate our lives. Jon sought not just to capture life's precious moments: He wanted to *create* those magical moments to capture.

Jon and I have been friends for nearly 20 years, and his character and philosophies have helped shape me into the person I am today. Eleven years ago, Jon started the Front Row Foundation, a charity that gives children and adults who have life-threatening illnesses an opportunity to attend the performance of their dreams, live in the front row.

What Jon did not know when he founded the Front Row Foundation is how the experiences he offered the recipients would change the world. The charity serves not only the recipients and their families, but also the teams who organize the events, the donors who support the Foundation, and the performers who see their work celebrated in the eyes of raving fans. Contribution converts the initial gift into a way of life. Living life in the front row means that, whatever seat you are given, you can always choose to make your life a front row experience.

Jon has collected what he has learned into the book you are reading now. *The Front Row Factor* will give you guiding questions so you can remain grounded in your day-to-day life. When you begin living life in the front row, you'll start asking questions that set you up to maximize every moment of your life. In the morning, you'll ask yourself,

How will I be a moment maker today?

During the day, you'll be asking,

How can I recognize or create a front row moment right now?

At the end of the day, you'll reflect and celebrate by asking,

What were my front row moments today?

By asking these simple questions, you'll shift your focus in a positive, empowering way, and living life in the front row will quickly become a *better* way of life!

I began supporting the Front Row Foundation before I wrote *The Miracle Morning* or created the Miracle Morning Community, so it was natural for me to allow the book and the community that grew up around it to support the charity as well. Jon gave me the gift of living my life in the front row, a gift I appreciate beyond measure. So, not only does 10 percent of the profits from each of my books sold go directly to the Foundation, but I am tremendously grateful that members of the Miracle Morning Community have raised or donated over $300,000 for the charity.

Life comes with unexpected twists and turns. Near the end of 2016, I was diagnosed with cancer. Although there have been many difficult days that tested my attitude of gratitude, I find I have deepened my reasons to live life in the front row. Now, every moment is a front row moment. Like any Front Row recipient, I didn't choose this cancer "seat," but I still have the choice to live my life in the front row. It is truly a way of life—one that is not easily shaken, and one I am grateful to embrace.

The Front Row Factor: Transform Your Life with the Art of Moment Making will give you the tools you need to become a moment maker for yourself and others. Jon has curated from the collected experiences of every Front Row recipient wisdom for how each of us can live our lives in the front row. He has eloquently written the nuggets of knowledge you need to know to transform any moment into an extraordinary one.

More than a book, you are holding an incredibly powerful tool that will unlock your ability to become a moment maker. I am grateful to have witnessed the magical moments that led to this book, and I cannot wait to witness the magical moments *you* create after you finish reading this heartfelt masterpiece. I invite you to join us in the front row; are you ready?

With gratitude,

Hal Elrod
Author of *The Miracle Morning*
www.MiracleMorning.com

MAKE THE MOST OF EVERY
MOMENT

Your problems are your problems and your challenges are your challenges, but you can live in the moment and be absorbed in the joy of life despite those challenges. You only have one shot at this. What are you going to do?

—JAKE BURKE, Father of Jack Burke, Front Row Recipient

I AM A MOMENT MAKER.

At age nine, I remember waking up before my parents rolled out of bed and hurrying downstairs just so I could design breakfast menus and clean up the living room. I was longing for my mom and dad to say, "Oh my gosh honey, you are the sweetest kid ever. You made my day."

I was addicted to making people feel good. Who doesn't crave the approval and love of their parents or those they care about most? I created moments for others that would fulfill my need for love, connection, significance, and even contribution. Naturally, we tend to give in ways which we personally value, and I was looking for ways to make people feel special.

In grade school, I had the biggest crush on a girl named Gina. For Valentine's Day, I gave her a bar of soap that I had carved with my Cub Scout knife into the shape of a heart. What's crazy is that 12 years later I ran into Gina and she said, "You're not going to believe this, but I still have that bar of soap." True story. In hindsight, it was stories like these that shaped my identity—*I am a moment maker*.

In my late 20s, I had an awesome job. I was a "moment maker" for a direct sales company where I traveled the world, worked with incredible people, and made good money. I was proud of my professional success and was having a blast. I was living the dream. *Almost*. At some point I realized something was missing. I was feeling grateful for my work, I just wasn't completely fulfilled. I was searching for a higher purpose and deeper meaning.

At age 29, I sat down with my journal and wrote:

What does ideal look like in all categories of my life: health, family, friends, spiritual, financial, and contribution?

I discovered that contribution was missing. I asked myself, *How would I make a difference in the world?* I wasn't sure exactly how to do this, or who I wanted to help, but I knew what I *did not* want to do: I didn't want to spend the first half of my life trying to get rich and fulfill my every desire and then spend the second half of my life figuring out how to give it away once I was stuffed to the gills with everything I wanted.

I've always been fascinated with the question, *How much do we need to thrive before we turn the focus to serving others?* For many of us, it's a lot less than we think.

The calling to contribute led to the start of the Front Row Foundation (FRF). The charity helps people fighting for their lives have a front row experience at the live event of their dreams. The Front Row Foundation is unique because of its philosophy. It's not just about making a dream come true for one day. It is about *how we can live every day in the front row.* Living life in the front row is a metaphor for getting close to what makes us come alive. It's about making the most of each moment, and the best moments are the ones we call *front row moments.*

The book you're holding now captures everything we've learned over the past 11 years.

I should add here that, throughout the book, when I write from the viewpoint of *we*, I'm talking about the Front Row family. The family is made up of staff, donors, supporters, those we serve, and anyone else connected to our cause.

It has been a *we* thing, not a *me* thing. I may be the one writing the book and telling you the story, but the wisdom I'm about to share has been the work of countless amazing people coming together to make a difference. In the acknowledgements section at the end of this book, you can read about the many incredible people, organizations and communities who've brought the Front Row Foundation to life.

LEARNING ABOUT LIFE

Although I started the Front Row Foundation as a way to give, I feel at times like I've been the biggest beneficiary. Each recipient has taught me so much. I've had a front row seat to see nearly 100 courageous individuals who've chosen to make the most of every moment, even under the most challenging circumstances.

I realized that over the years I was learning how to live life from those fighting for it.

Steve Jobs, the legendary founder of Apple, once said, "All external expectations, all pride, all fear of embarrassment or failure—these things just fall away in the face of death, leaving only what is truly important."

For you and me, any moment could be our last. That's not meant to be depressing; it's meant to inspire you to make the most of the time you have.

***Now* counts.**

Knowing it could all end at any moment, I've come to understand the power of asking *How can I make the most of this moment?*

Your life, from beginning to end, is simply a series of many moments, one after another, until it's over. You continually create and give meaning to each of these moments.

My guess is that you're reading this because you want to live a great life full of great moments.

I've been taught that if we want to achieve a big goal such as living an epic life, we must look to the end and reverse-engineer it from there so we understand what needs to happen now. Here's how it looks.

A great life is stringing together as many great years as possible.

A great year is 12 great months.

A great month is 30 great days.

A great day is 24 great hours.

A great hour is making every minute count.

A great minute occurs when each passing moment is experienced to the fullest.

With every passing moment, your life story is being written.

That is why this moment matters.

If you follow this logic, the very next thought, comment, question, or other action you take is vital to living a life with purpose and meaning.

You're never fully in control of what happens to you, but you are absolutely, 100 percent in control of *what it means* and therefore *how it feels*.

And the quality of your life is largely determined by how you feel the majority of the time. How we feel is rooted in our focus, which is determined by the questions we ask. When we ask, *How can we make the most of each and every moment?* . . . our brains start searching for the answer.

The art of moment making is *creatively taking all that surrounds you, good or bad, and intentionally making the most of it for yourself and others.*

MY PROMISE

In the pages ahead, we've decoded what it takes to make the most of each and every moment in your life. That's a big promise, I know, and I don't say it lightly. Even my editor as we're writing this book said, *I think you've found the secret to living.* It's not meant to be overly dramatic; I simply believe it 100 percent.

I do believe this book can absolutely change your life by helping you make the most of each and every moment. I want your investment of time, energy, and money to pay off for you and all those you love in huge ways.

I'm motivated to honor our recipients and to serve you. I'm also aware that one day my kids will read this. The words on the following pages are the ones I want my boys to read. When I'm gone, this will be one of my greatest gifts to them.

This book is filled with compelling stories and proven strategies, and backed by fascinating science. I'm going to show you how to cultivate a *front row mindset* so you can handle anything life throws at you. I'll give you ideas on forming *meaningful relationships* with anyone you encounter. I'll present proven approaches to help you *shape your environment* to give you the best possible chance at winning the game of life. I'll demonstrate the misunderstood and overlooked power of *hope for the future, living in the moment,* and *celebrating our past experiences.* I'll do all this by sharing the true stories of our recipients and my own life experiences. I'll show you the way and give you actionable steps so you can embrace the art of moment making today.

So now that you have a front row seat, let's get on with the show.

A FRONT ROW LIFE

PART ONE

What lies behind us and what lies ahead of us are tiny matters compared to what lies within us.

—HENRY STANLEY HASKINS

A DEEPER MEANING

Invest in yourself and others.

CHAPTER ONE

The purpose of life is to serve, and to show the compassion and the will to help others.

—ALBERT SCHWEITZER

AFTER A FEW YEARS OF HAVING MY DREAM job, I still had a nagging feeling that something was missing. My job allowed me to take sales champions to the nicest restaurants and get them into the hottest clubs in Vegas, but I wasn't entirely fulfilled and was looking for something else. I was craving a higher purpose and deeper meaning in my life.

Lying in bed late one night, I saw a Tony Robbins infomercial. He was selling his audio program *Personal Power*. I thought to myself, *Oh yeah ... you can "totally transform your health, wealth, blah blah blah" for only $200. Are there really people who fall for this?*

But then I also wondered, *Can one guy really help me? Is this Tony Robbins guy just getting rich off people hoping for a better life? Infomercials don't sell quality stuff, right?* The fact is, I really needed to change. I listened to his message. I felt like Tony was speaking directly to me when he talked about living to your fullest potential.

Then my thoughts went to, *I wonder if this actually works for people. What if Tony is for real? What if the CDs are worth $200?*

"What creates an extraordinary life," Tony said, "is an extraordinary mindset, an extraordinary psychology, where you don't settle, where you're unreasonable in your expectations of yourself, where you say, 'I'm going to defy all the limitations, I'm going to defy my background, I'm going to defy all the people who say it can't be done, and I'm going to step up.'"

Yes! I had been settling. I wasn't unreasonable with expectations of myself. I wasn't pushing the limits, and I hadn't truly stepped up. I was ready for the next level, and I was looking for strategies and motivation to level up my life. But I wasn't quite there yet. Tony made learning sound fun, exciting, and relevant to my life. He helped me understand *why* I did what I did and how my brain works.

"Until you get honest with yourself,"
he said, "you can't change."

I had been lying to myself for years about who I was, what I was capable of, and what I wanted. Eventually, this thought hit me: *Whether those CDs are worth $200 or not, you know what? I am worth $200 to find out. Even if the CDs are total garbage, what's the worst that can happen? But wait ... what if the CDs are awesome ... what's the best that can happen?*

I bought Tony Robbins Personal Power for $200. More importantly, I took action—just like you did in buying and reading this book. I listened every day in my car while I was driving to and from work, and my life started to change. In fact, I remember someone saying,

"Jon, you're so much more interesting
when you're focused on learning."

This lit me up. People could sense the change in my energy, and they liked it. I improved my physical health, improved my finances, gained control of my life with better time management, strengthened relationships, deepened my impact through work, and developed a spiritual awareness. What first set that in motion was when I decided that I, Jon Vroman, was worth $200. The program helped me uncover a more authentic version of me. I originally thought the CDs were all about me thriving, but I found out it was more than that. Tony talked about helping others. A truly epic life involves giving at the highest levels.

I remember Tony asking, "On a 1–10 scale, where would you rate your contribution to the world?" This question is what sparked my desire to give. I was missing the feeling of genuine contribution. Listening to his CDs helped bring the giving conversation into focus. The more I learned, the more I had to share. In the beginning, I asked:

How can I help myself?

My new question became:

*How can I help myself **and** others?*

This was the first major step toward living in the front row of my life. From that day, I pursued personal growth *and* contribution with intensity and focus. I'm not known for moderation. I'm all in, or I'm out. Making the decision to invest in myself would be one of the elements needed to start, build, and grow the Front Row Foundation.

How would you like to contribute to the world?

LIFE IS DIFFERENT IN THE FRONT ROW

You might not choose your seat, but you can always choose a front row experience.

Remember that you are always exactly where you need to be, experiencing what you need to experience so that you can learn what you must learn in order to become the person you need to be to create everything you want for your life. Always.

—HAL ELROD, Founder of *TheMiracleMorning.com*

I LOVED THE BACK ROW. SEATS ARE LESS expensive, you don't have to fight crowds to get to the bathroom, and when the show is over, it's easier to get to your car. In the back, you can see everybody, and no one can see you. It feels safe. One could argue it's practical. What I'd soon learn was that, while inexpensive, the back row still comes at a cost.

In 2005, when I attended a Jason Mraz concert at the Kimmel Center for the Performing Arts in Philadelphia, per usual, I felt very comfortable as I took my seat in the balcony, in the very last row. It was my birthday and, with my girlfriend by my side, it was a great night.

The venue seats 650 people—it was intimate. I couldn't help but notice that the four girls in the front row were having an amazing time. They were singing, dancing, and throwing their hands in the air while shouting out song requests to Jason.

I looked around at the people sitting in the nosebleed section with me. It was a totally different energy. They seemed to be checked out, as if they were counting the minutes rather than making the most of each one. Their body language spoke loud and clear: *I want to be anywhere but here.* When I looked back to the front, I noticed that those women seemed to feel the opposite:

I want to be here and nowhere else.

My teenage self would have said, "Wow, those people are so lucky to get those seats." My slightly more evolved self asked, "I wonder how those people got those seats?" Once I asked the question, I thought of some possibilities.

Maybe they camped through the night to hold their spot in line. Maybe they have great connections. Maybe they had the money to pay top dollar. Maybe they didn't even have front row tickets but saw open seats and took them.

By the end of the show I decided that, however they got there, one thing was clear: They wanted a front row seat, a front row experience, and they went after it.

In my life, I could see certain areas where I was settling for whatever seat came my way. I knew I'd chosen the back row in my relationships, my career, my health, and other areas of life. I had reached a certain level of comfort and security in life. Yet I couldn't shake the question, *What else is there?* For many like myself, it starts with survival: How much do you need to pay rent, get a car, and buy food? Then you start to think about a nicer place, a fancier car, and eating out. Eventually, if you keep going, you find your way to the pursuit of a higher purpose and deeper meaning. This is what Maslow figured out in 1943 when he spoke about a five-tier model of human needs:

We start with physiological needs like food and water. If those needs are met, we focus on safety. Third is relationships, which is followed by the fourth tier—feeling like you're accomplishing things. Finally, the top tier is self-actualization of your fullest potential. I kept asking myself, *What is my fullest potential? What does a front row life look like?*

GRATEFUL

As we reach for full potential, it's important to remain grateful. On a recent podcast interview with my friend Ryland Engelhart, co-owner of Cafe Gratitude, he said, "Ask for what you want, be grateful for what you get."

We can all be grateful for what we have while we pursue what we want.

Gratitude is not complacency. I'm grateful for all the back row moments of life. In many ways, they provide contrast for my front row experiences. If I'd never experienced life in the back row, I might not fully appreciate the front. And the back isn't always bad; it offers wonderful perspective you don't get up front. I once saw Cirque du Soleil in Vegas, and there was so much going on—people swinging from the ceiling and climbing on walls. For that show, it's arguable that the back was as interesting as the front because you had a wider view of everything happening.

On the night of the Mraz show, I felt grateful for my seat in the balcony (still do—I wouldn't be writing this book if I hadn't been there), but I also wanted to make sure that the next time I saw him I was intentional about my seat and, most importantly, that I would level up my experience.

> If you don't like your seat, change it.
>
> If you can't change it, make the most of it.
>
> You might not choose your seat in life, but you can always choose to have a front row experience.

WHAT DOES A FRONT ROW LIFE LOOK LIKE TO YOU?

ULTRA-PURPOSE

When your *why* has a heart, your *how* gets legs.

When you're surrounded by people who share a passionate commitment around a common purpose, anything is possible.

—HOWARD SCHULTZ, CEO of Starbucks

ONE HOT SUMMER DAY, SEVERAL WEEKS AFTER THE Jason Mraz concert, my buddy Jamie Baugher and I decided we should run an ultramarathon. We gave ourselves only 16 weeks to train. It was what I called the *season of yes*, which was all about pushing the limits and seeing what I was made of.

After Jamie and I committed, I let my girlfriend know about the run. Since I needed to start training immediately, I told her "I'm going for a run until my feet bleed so I can see what I'm made of." I left our house with spirits high, humming the tune of *Rocky* in my head (okay, probably out loud).

As it turns out, I was made of 3.7 miles.

Even if you've never run a marathon before, you can probably grasp how nuts this timeline was. We're talking couch to 50-mile marathon in four months. It would be physically grueling, and I had to overcome *the story* that I wasn't a runner. Was this even possible? If it was, I needed every possible tool, resource, and hack to pull this off.

The first thing I needed to do was change the question I was asking myself. I needed to turn, "*Can* we run 52.4 miles in sixteen weeks?" into "*How can we* run 52.4 miles in sixteen weeks?"

WHEN YOUR WHY HAS HEART, YOUR HOW GETS LEGS

About two weeks into the process, Jamie and I set out on our longest training run. We ran the eight-mile loop in Fairmount Park, which sits on the banks of the Schuylkill River in Philadelphia. Energetic people ran the trails and rowed on the river. It was a gorgeous day, and I had the company of my good friend.

When you're running with someone for 90 minutes, you've got plenty of time to talk. We decided that we wanted our ultramarathon to count for something more than sore legs. We would use our project to raise money for charity. *Yes!* We both agreed this was a great idea, but what charity? We ran through a list of possibilities, citing pros and cons. Then we asked, "What if we designed the ideal charity? What would that look like?"

We considered what we were passionate about, but then dug a little deeper. Oftentimes, motivation to give and serve comes from what we fear and what we love, two of the greatest driving forces for any human being. So I asked myself, *What do I fear and what do I love?*

I feared being insignificant and unimportant, not mattering. I also feared disconnection: Getting to the end of my life only to realize I had never lived. I was terrified of not fully living to my full potential. I feared failing to make the most of each day and wasting whatever time I was given.

What I love most are experiences I'll never forget. I love concerts, travel, once-in-a-lifetime moments. I love celebrating what's great in life, making other people smile, and helping them feel fully alive. I love making moments count.

It was in *that moment* that these words rolled off my tongue:

We decided that we wanted to create our own charity that puts people fighting for their lives in the front row of a live event of their dreams. That was it! This was the higher purpose I was looking for! Our decision immediately brought a deeper meaning to my life.

Something else unexpected happened in the moment of decision. The second we turned the conversation to serving others, miraculously, I wasn't tired anymore. I found the source of true energy: **contribution**. As we ran, I forgot about my feet, my legs, and the sweat pouring off my head. I had a new fuel. It was **purpose**.

ULTRA-DAY

The day of our ultramarathon came on a cold November morning. Jamie and I laced up our running shoes at his house and set out for Long Beach Island. We felt confident even though, up to that moment, the farthest I had run in training was 17 miles—and I was setting out to complete 52.4 miles.

At about mile 13, I was already tired, so Jamie and I started a walk-run strategy. We'd run for 10 minutes, then walk for one. We experimented with many strategies that day. One of the most powerful was setting small goals. Jamie would say "See that telephone pole down the road? We're going to run to that and take a breather."

With each goal achieved, we'd celebrate. Then we'd set another target, run to it, and celebrate. We'd high-five each other then set another goal. We pressed on.

At mile 26, my knee was screaming. I could barely walk, let alone run. We were six hours into the day, and I'll never forget the moment I stopped completely and sat on the ground. I was almost in tears when I looked at my leg and said, "OK leg, I know you're hurting. I hear you, but listen, we need to finish this. I need you to be strong. We told so many of our friends that we're raising money for the Front Row Foundation, and I realize this is tough, but nothing we go through today will come close to the pain our recipients experience on a daily basis. So it's time to go."

And go we did. One painful step after another, we made it to Long Beach Island, New Jersey. Looking back, we made it through those 15 hours because of three strategies.

First, we **managed the moment**. We took one moment at a time and dealt with the obstacle directly in front of us. If we'd thought about all the challenges to come, I don't think we would have been successful.

Second, we **set small goals**. We didn't think about running 52 miles, we thought about running one mile, 52 times.

Third, we **celebrated our progress**, rather than waiting until the end. We didn't get caught up in what was wrong or hard. We focused on what was going right, over and over again. Each goal reached was cause for celebration.

Approaching our day in this way allowed us to gain momentum. Our mantra was, "Keep moving." Above all, we had purpose. The higher purpose of contribution provided a deeper meaning for the run and that pulled us forward.

Our finish line was the oceanfront, and as I sat in the sand that night I felt like a champion. A new Jon Vroman had been born.

CONNECTING THE DOTS

I'm often asked about what led to the start of Front Row Foundation. In hindsight, I can connect the dots of three very important moments.

The first was choosing to invest in myself with the Tony Robbins CDs. What began as *How can I make my life better?* quickly expanded to *How can I make other people's lives better?* Tony didn't just challenge me to improve my life, he taught me the importance of service.

The second moment was the Jason Mraz concert. I realized that life was different in the front row. I decided that I needed to show up, step up, and speak up if I wanted a more fulfilling experience of life.

The third moment, choosing to run a 52.4-mile ultramarathon, led to the question *How could we integrate purpose into our pursuit?* We found power through purpose. The minute I found this, I knew there was so much more to the run than just crossing the finish line. Getting clear about wanting to serve others *as I was striving for success* would lead to the birth of the Front Row Foundation.

HOW WILL YOU BRING MORE PURPOSE AND MEANING INTO YOUR LIFE?

FRONT ROW FOUNDATION

Learning about life from those fighting for it.

Most people overestimate what they can do in one year and underestimate what they can do in ten years.

—BILL GATES

I'VE NOTICED IN MY LIFE A PATTERN:

I get inspired.
I start something.
I fail.
I'm confused.
I learn.
I grow.
I connect the dots.
I tell the story.
Others benefit.

This is how I would sum up the story of the Front Row Foundation. Looking back over a decade of helping people experience life in the front row, I would never have predicted the stories, outcomes, and lessons I'm about to share in the following chapters. Today, I can say with absolute certainty that the Front Row Foundation has transformed my life and the lives of many others.

Before we get into all that we learned, I'll share four transformational moments in the Front Row Foundation history so this entire story makes sense.

THE FIRST TRANSFORMATIONAL MOMENT:
OUR FIRST FRONT ROW EXPERIENCE

In February 2006, just a few months after the ultramarathon, we hosted our first front row experience. Effie Huboky was an energetic, honest, beautiful, and caring woman: a friend's mom who lived in Pennsylvania. Effie loved going to the Jersey Shore, and when she wasn't working hard as a bank manager, enjoyed boat rides and picnic lunches. She was fiercely loyal and would do anything for her loved ones.

Effie had experienced health problems her whole life. Born with half-sized kidneys that couldn't keep up with the demands of her growing body, in 1982 Effie received a kidney transplant. She lived normally for many years, but fell ill in 1999 as her body started to reject the transplant. Aside from kidney issues, she also fought hepatitis C and liver disease. Despite the challenges she faced, Effie remained optimistic.

Her husband, John, said the family was absolutely thrilled when the Front Row Foundation asked her to be its first recipient. John said, "Effie loves country-western music she can dance to." Our staff went to work and secured front row tickets to a Brooks & Dunn concert. Effie and John arrived at the event in a stretch limo and had an incredible dinner before the show.

When they arrived at the venue, Effie and John approached the will-call window to pick up their tickets. The woman who was helping them looked at the location of the seats and said, "Wow! I don't know who you know to have gotten these seats, but you must be somebody very important!"

At the end of that evening, Effie said, "I had the time of my life. The thrill of sitting in the front row watching their performance is something I'll never forget." She wrote to us,

"To say thank you just seems so inadequate for all the time and effort that has been donated by everyone to make this experience possible."

Dear Front Row Foundation,

I had the time of my life at the Brooks & Dunn concert with my husband John. The thrill of sitting in the front row watching their performance, is something to remember. Their show lasted two wonderful hours. I was able to purchase a hat and receive their autograph. I was a real cowgirl ... How cool is that?

To say thank you just seems so inadequate for all the time and effort that has been donated by everyone to make this experience possible.

The vision of the FRF is to make dreams come true and you certainly have done that for me!

Fondly,
Effie Hulohy

Several years after Effie passed away, we caught up with John, who shared with us that "She never forgot that evening."

Effie's front row experience was a transformative moment for everyone involved because we witnessed the power we all had to positively influence someone's life.

THE SECOND TRANSFORMATIONAL MOMENT:

OUR FIRST COMMUNITY FUNDRAISER

Knowing we'd need to raise money for future recipients, we planned to hold a "Beef & Beer" fundraiser in the local fire hall just down the road from my house. A small group of friends came together and sat around the kitchen table to plan the big day. We laughed, created, and divvied up tasks. These were exciting times spent with great people who were fueled by a deep desire to make a difference.

On the day of the fundraiser, 220 of our friends showed up, and we raised around $20,000, which included a check for $8,888.88 that my incredible friend Jon Berghoff quietly handed to me. I'll never forget how I felt when I held that check. His generosity inspired me.

I was moved by all the people stepping up big for the Front Row Foundation that night. I could see the power of our friends coming together with a shared purpose. We were defining our values, acting with courage, and serving others. This felt great.

We no longer wished for a better community:
We were making one.

THE THIRD TRANSFORMATIONAL MOMENT:

FOCUSING MY PROFESSIONAL LIFE TO SERVE THE CHARITY

My appetite to serve the Front Row Foundation was growing. But as an employee working 9–5, I had limited time to invest in the charity. Instead of asking myself, *How can I make more time during evenings and weekends?* I decided to ask, *If I were to design my ideal life, how could I do work that would allow me the freedom to focus on the Front Row Foundation as much as I wanted?*

After some deep soul-searching, it became clear that my professional life wasn't aligning with my newly defined core value of service. Although I worked with awesome people at an incredible company, made great money, traveled the world, and had the best boss ever, I continued exploring questions about my purpose for being here. The more I asked questions like *Why am I here?* the more I saw that my current work wasn't working.

So I started asking three very powerful new questions:

1. ***What are my superpowers?*** **I see this as our best natural talents.**

2. *What are my passions?* I see this as what lights us up.

3. *Who can I help?* I see this as the person or group we most want to serve.

My soul-searching led me to take a leap of faith and become an entrepreneur. In 2008, I decided to make a bold move and become a full-time speaker, coach, and author. I set out in search of higher purpose and deeper meaning in my work and personal life.

Several months into my entrepreneurial journey, I attended a mastermind meeting, which consisted of a small group of business owners who gathered to help one another. I shared with everyone that I wasn't sure what my focus, brand, and overall business strategy should be. How could I make money while keeping my focus on the Front Row Foundation?

The six people around the table all looked at me as if the answer was obvious. With one voice, they said, "Front Row Everything!" They enthusiastically explained that I could help people live life in the front row through speaking, coaching, books, and hosting other live events that would bring attention, funds, and connections to the charity.

They hit the nail on the head. Today, for example, each time I take the stage for a keynote presentation, I talk about the charity. Because of this, countless people have approached me to say something like, "Hey Jon, if you ever need tickets for your recipients, just say the word." We've made connections that have given us access to front row seats we would never be able to secure otherwise, not to mention that it's saved our charity thousands of dollars from not having to purchase them.

As Aaron Hurst wrote in *The Purpose Economy*, "Purpose isn't a cause; it is an approach to work and serving others. Purpose is a verb, not a noun." I started obsessing over how my business could have more soul. Simply aiming to make a profit seemed to miss something. As I researched further, I found an entire community focused around creating purpose-driven businesses.

In the book *Firms of Endearment*, authors Rajendra S. Sisodia, David B. Wolfe, and Jagdish N. Sheth tracked companies that operated with purpose over the period of 1996–2006. Those organizations with a "soul," whose founders believe in doing good while doing well, outperformed the S&P 500 by more than an 8-to-1 ratio.[1] Over the years, I've been drawn to companies like Tom's Shoes, which donates a pair every time one is purchased, or Patagonia, whose mission is: *Build the best product, cause no unnecessary harm, use business to inspire, and implement solutions to the environmental crisis.* If you're a business owner or thinking about becoming one, consider this wisdom shared by the great business strategist Michael Porter and his co-author Mark Kramer: "Businesses must reconnect company success with social progress."[2]

The third transformational moment was discovering that I could help people live life in the front row professionally, and that by doing so it would directly serve the charity. Creating a business with a social impact was giving me a deep sense of purpose. I was becoming a social entrepreneur.

A great example of this synergy is the book you're holding in your hands. A portion of the sales from each book go directly to the charity. By reading this book and sharing it, you not only help others live life in the front row, you also help us create our next front row experience.

THE FOURTH TRANSFORMATIVE MOMENT:

LEARNING HOW TO LIVE LIFE FROM THOSE FIGHTING FOR IT

Over the past 11 years of creating nearly 100 front row experiences, I've noticed something magical happening. Looking back now it seems so obvious, but when we first started out it wasn't on my radar. Initially, our one mission was clear—to create an unforgettable experience for someone in need. What we never saw coming was that the impact of one event was fueled by three very powerful forces.

Hope. When we told someone they were going to experience the live event of their dreams, we noticed a shift in their mindset immediately. **Hope brings the future into the present moment and makes *now* better.** It wasn't just about one day at the event, it was about every day leading up to it. During difficult times, we gain strength through hope—knowing our lives can be different tomorrow. It's energizing to know that spring always follows winter. I believe the more we find power in *now*, the better *then* will be.

Celebration: After the front row experience, we noticed recipients and their families celebrating in the months and years following. It wasn't just about one front row day, it was about bringing that feeling with us and using its power to live every day in the front row. **When we celebrate our past experiences, we bring back positive emotions, which make *now* better.** We find strength when we recall past obstacles we've conquered. Celebration is about amplifying what's good, and silencing what's not.

Presence: To have a great life, we must learn to make the most of each moment. Choosing our present focus determines how we feel. Our thoughts are like a pendulum that sways from the past to the future; becoming present is about finding the center. I want to remember my past, dream about tomorrow, and feel each of those while consciously living in the moment. **Life is happening now.** Being a moment maker is about making the most of now.

I've noticed that these three forces of hope, celebration, and presence—ultimately, living in the moment—are the key forces at work in helping recipients and families, as well as being the key forces for anyone who wants to live a front row life. Let's take a deeper dive into each of these forces and talk about how they can help you make the most of each and every moment, starting today.

WHAT HAVE BEEN

THE BIGGEST

AND BEST

MOMENTS OF

YOUR LIFE?

THREE FORCES AT WORK

PART
TWO

Don't fight forces, use them.

—BUCKMINSTER FULLER

HOPE FOR THE FUTURE

What makes you come alive?

CHAPTER FIVE

Hope is a good thing, maybe the best of things,
and no good thing ever dies.

—STEPHEN KING, *The Shawshank Redemption*

WHEN I'M TUCKING MY SON INTO BED AT night, we'll talk about all the fun things we can do the next day. This is especially effective when he might be experiencing some fear of the dark or monsters under the bed. I learned the magic of redirection from my mother-in-law, Tamara. By shifting the focus, she can instantly shift the emotional experience for our kids. By asking my son what he is most looking forward to tomorrow, it seems to bring a smile to his face, and often he'll forget about his fears.

"Tomorrow, let's make pancakes," I'll say.

He'll reply, "Tomorrow is going to be the best day ever!"

I see him light up with the anticipation of maple syrup coursing through his veins. The cool thing is that his focus on the future brings joy to the present moment. That's not avoiding our reality, that's shaping it.

People need hope.

MEET FRONT ROW RECIPIENT JACK BURKE

Eight-year old Jack Burke went to see the world's greatest magic show for his front row experience. Jack was born with a genetic disorder called Neurofibromatosis (NF); a condition where tumors continually form and grow, both internally and externally. Treatment is surgical but often includes chemotherapy, which is what happened to Jack after a tumor was found on his brain stem. His selfless nature and sweet smile make him impossible not to love. In fact, he started a charity, Cure NF with Jack, that has raised more than one million dollars. He leaves melted hearts wherever he goes. When Jack was 8 years old, the Front Row Foundation team sent Jack and his family to see *the world's greatest magic show*.

> You can see Jack's photos and video at:
> www.frontrowfoundation.org/jack-burke/

Jack is like many of our recipients. When he found out he was going to the magic show, it ignited a bright light of hope and anticipation during a difficult time. That power in the present given by hope for the future was contagious amongst the whole Burke family. I hope the admirable nature of Jack's choice to have a TGIF attitude even when Friday meant chemo is similarly inspiring for you, too.

During an interview following his experience, Jack's father told us this:

"Above all is the hope that is woven through your life. If you don't have that, then you're in trouble."

Think about that word, "hope." I've used the word many times, but failed to truly understand its meaning or impact until writing this book. Dr. Shane Lopez, former senior scientist at Gallup and author of *Making Hope Happen: Create the Future You Want for Yourself and Others* says that hope is "the belief that the future will be better than the present," along with the belief that you have the power to make it so.[3]

Hope brings the power of the future into the present moment.

MEET FRONT ROW RECIPIENT MELISSA WEAVER

Recipient Melissa Weaver is a licensed clinical social worker by trade and a lifeline to those who seek her for counseling.

She is also wife to Suzi Weaver and mother to daughters Juliet and Isabel. In August, 2013, Melissa was diagnosed with an aggressive type of breast cancer called Invasive Ductal Carcinoma (Stage 2). It is no secret to friends and family that Melissa is a huge, longtime fan of Sarah McLachlan. At several pivotal points during her life, Melissa has leaned on and gained strength from Sarah McLachlan's music. After months of planning, Front Row Foundation was able to take Melissa to see McLachlan live in concert. Not only did she sit in the front row during the show, she was actually taken up onto the stage.

> Read more about Melissa's story at:
> www.frontrowfoundation.org/melissa-weaver/

Melissa credits her front row event with changing, even saving, her life:

Front Row helped save my life. I know that sounds overly sentimental, but it's actually the truth. When I say that, what I mean is Front Row has created a new perspective on how to embrace life—I needed that. I needed that at a time when I had to grab onto and believe in something. I needed something to keep me going each day. That's what Front Row has done.

———

Other recipients and their family members have shared with us about the emotional transformation that occurs before, during, and after their front row experience. We've seen it repeatedly: Hope changes your outlook, which changes how you feel, and this changes what you do in the moment. Hope creates positive energy.

MEET FRONT ROW RECIPIENT GEOFF MCLEOD

Geoff McLeod—"Big Red" to his friends—is an inspiration to many. He is a true giver in the community. Whether he's expressing his passions for nature, wildlife, rugby, or Crossfit, he's all in. He didn't just play rugby; he was the president of the Northern Saskatchewan Rugby Union. He didn't just do crossfit; he competed in and judged competitions. He doesn't just love wildlife; he's the president of the Saskatchewan Wildlife Rehabilitation Society.

On May 29, 2013, the McLeods (Geoff's wife of four years and their two daughters Grace and Bethany) discovered that Geoff had stage 4 Glioblastoma—inoperable brain tumors.

After Geoff was selected to be a Front Row recipient, the event coordinators were able to locate tickets to see his favorite hockey team, the Detroit Red Wings. Not only would Geoff be seeing a game—on his birthday, I might add—he was allowed to attend the team's practice in the morning and then have lunch with the team.

His wife, Jamille, shared how life changed at their home in the time leading up to the game:

It was something to look forward to, which was fantastic. That was huge for us. Around that we received tons of support, positive people, and lots of love. Up to that point, Geoff had been getting worse and worse. It was harder to get into his wheelchair, and he wasn't even getting out of bed at certain times. When we had the goal of his front row event in front of us, he improved and improved and improved to the point where not only did we have him in a wheelchair, but he also could get up and walk. Anticipating the event seemed to pick him up. We had this big thing to look forward to, get ready for, and be well for, so it was really good that way.

———

I can't say for sure whether Geoff would have made such progress without his game to look forward to, but I've noticed time and time again that positive anticipation provides the fuel to attempt the extraordinary when we would otherwise refrain, which is applicable no matter your circumstances.

WHEN YOU BRING PURPOSE TO THE PRESENT MOMENT THROUGH HOPE, YOU BRING POWER.

What our recipients have said aligns with *expectancy theory*, an idea coined by Victor Vroom of the Yale School of Management. The basic concept is that the brain acts on what it thinks will happen next. Dr. Marcel Kinsbourne, a neuroscientist at the New School for Social Research in New York, says that expectations create brain patterns that can be just as real as those created by events in the real world. Expectations cause neurons to fire, which tips the nervous system to trigger physical responses. Similarly Shawn Achor, a happiness researcher and the author of *The Happiness Advantage*, says, "The mental construction of our daily activities, more than the activity itself, defines our reality." Every time we'd reveal to a recipient that they were going to the event of their dreams, we'd immediately see the power of positive expectancy and its potential to reshape their current reality.

MEET FRONT ROW RECIPIENT ELLA JOY WON

Ella Joy is an outgoing and witty little girl who is a surprisingly gifted conversationalist and loves to be in the spotlight. She adores Disney princesses and all things science, loves collecting gems and rocks, and enjoys reading, dancing, crafting, singing, and playing at the park with her younger brother. She brings joy to every room she enters, and she brings smiles to every face she meets. Her family is her everything.

One day, Ella's Mom was tickling her and noticed a walnut-sized lump on her leg. After one appointment with their pediatrician and two subsequent meetings with pediatric surgeons, the family received word from a biopsy procedure: Ella Joy had stage 4 non-Hodgkin lymphoma cancer (T-cell).

Ella loves all things Disney and has always dreamed of seeing a **live** "Disney on Ice" performance. Her dream came true when the Front Row event coordinators showed up at her house with a black stretch limousine to take her and her family for their front row experience. Dressed from head to toe in full princess attire and immersed in the experience of skating Disney characters all around her, Ella had the time of her life that day!

> See more at:
> www.frontrowfoundation.org/ella-joy-won/

Her mom Anne shared this with our team:

It gave us a lot of hope because, when you have a child with cancer, I think that sometimes it's easy to look at the present situation and think about all the stresses and the worries and the unknown. When you have something to look forward to, and for us that was Disney on Ice, it gave us something else to focus on, not the medical aspect and "Is she taking her chemo meds today?"—all that. We could focus on something happy and exciting.

We know that many of our recipients have fears about their current health situation. Our recipients and their families shared that they sometimes struggle deciding which doctors they should listen to. They fear and worry how they will pay for treatments. They question what will happen to their family if something happens to them. We've seen that in times of struggle, hope provides light even in the darkest days, not just for our recipients, but for every family member. The power of hope extends into the communities of our recipients, and we certainly feel it within our team.

MEET FRONT ROW RECIPIENT RACHEL LITTMAN

No matter who you talk to, you will hear the same three things about Rachel Littman: "First, she's a fighter; second,

Rachel is determined; and third, she is inspiring." Born six minutes before her twin, Eva, Rachel was diagnosed with Familial Dysautonomia (FD), a progressive and ultimately fatal genetic disorder. There's currently no cure, symptoms vary widely, and the mean life span is 40 years. Looking at Rachel and her warm glowing smile, no one would ever know the daily struggles she faces with feeding tubes, poor muscle tone, developmental delays, fainting, and other challenges. When Rachel found out she was going to be a Front Row Foundation recipient, she was so shocked she could hardly speak. She and her family were flown to Hollywood to watch a live taping of her favorite show, *The Big Bang Theory*!

> Find out more about Rachel's experience at:
> www.frontrowfoundation.org/rachel-littman/

Rachel's mother, Robin, had this to say about her front row experience:

When the day came in which we revealed it to her, the expression on [Rachel's] face was priceless. She was speechless, and my daughter's never speechless. It was one of those moments, and it's possibly hard for people to understand who don't have children with chronic medical conditions, how rarely these wonderful moments come along. Usually there's a drudgery of dealing with certain aspects of your life that other people don't have to deal with, and some of it is just getting through each day in a healthy manner. To have something so unexpected, something that would take you out of that drudgery and out of the stress and the tension of living with managing all these medical needs and whatnot, you could just see her entire spirit lifted up as I read this letter to her. That set in motion a change in her that continues to this day.

———

Much like our recipients, you've probably experienced how hope has played an important role in your life. Having hope not only inspires us with a new vision for the future, but it helps us deal with our fears by redirecting our focus.

It's important to note that there's a difference between wishful thinking and being hopeful.

> **Wishful thinking says,**
> **"I wish something were different,"**
> **while hope says,**
> **"I'm going to make the difference."**

Dr. Shane Lopez, the psychologist and author mentioned earlier, suggests that the most hopeful people are often also the most realistic people. Those who are hopeful are often aware of challenges before they even happen and already have a plan to jump the hurdle, which is very different from wishing that the circumstances were different.

MEET FRONT ROW RECIPIENT LOGAN LAY

Logan loves to laugh and be silly. She is an extremely compassionate, caring girl and loves being with her friends. She adores kids and kids love her. She's into all types of music and art. In 2005 Logan was diagnosed with a Disseminated Astrocytoma/glioma of the brainstem and spine. Despite years of chemotherapy and several surgeries, Logan has relapsed three times. Logan has been told that she will likely spend the rest of her life trying to live in harmony with her tumor and managing all of the health issues she has.

Logan has gone through so much in her life and continues to fight each day with so many health issues, yet she never ever complains. She just takes everything in stride and continues to stay strong. Her family has actually never once heard her be negative or ask, *Why me?* She just continues to adjust.

Our team created a front row experience at the show of Logan's choosing (I can't reveal the event because of confidentiality agreements). Her mother, Jennifer Montgomery Lay, explained what anticipation of the event did for Logan and their family:

Here was this one cool thing we could look forward to and get excited about. It's really going to happen! It was something on the horizon that was hopeful, something fun to look forward to, and something completely unexpected. The experience lifted the gray fog of Logan's illness, and we felt like, "This is incredible, I can't believe this is going to happen for our family."

———————

I think it also gave us a little bit of a shift into possibility. That you don't always see how your future will unfold. Or what's possible even when you're in a dark place. When we had this to look forward to, suddenly we felt this little bit of letting go. We trusted that good things could happen. It was this kind of transition, we'd see each other in the hallway and say, "We're going to the show! High five!"

Hope pulls the power of the future into the present moment and crushes fear by shifting attention to the positive. Good and bad exist in each moment; we must choose which one gets our time, energy, and focus. From my experience and through countless conversations with recipients and their family members, I've discovered that without hope, our fears run wild and paralyze us. With hope, we are fueled with energy of possibility and moved to action.

What dreams make you come alive?

CELEBRATE OUR EXPERIENCES

What are your "front row" moments?

CHAPTER SIX

People of our time are losing the power of celebration.
Instead of celebrating we seek to be amused or entertained.
Celebration is an active state, an act of expressing reverence
or appreciation. To be entertained is a passive state—it is to receive
pleasure afforded by an amusing act or a spectacle ... Celebration is a
confrontation, giving attention to the transcendent meaning of one's actions.

—ABRAHAM JOSHUA HESCHEL

SOMEONE ONCE ASKED ME, "IS CELEBRATION ABOUT THE past, present, or future?" The answer is yes. Celebration is amplification. My friend Bailey Reagan, who just got her master's degree in Positive Psychology and helped with the research we've shared in this book, said this about celebration, "It is about looking forward to something in the future, intensifying the present moment, or reflecting on positive experiences from the the past." She often refers to celebration as *savoring*.

Celebration focuses our energy, usually with other people, on something positive we want to highlight. For this chapter, we're going to focus specifically on celebrating past experiences.

Each night at dinner, I ask my son Tiger, "What were your front row moments today?" Our family defines our front row moments as the highlights of the day. I also ask, "What was one failure you experienced, and what did you learn from it?" No matter what happens, we can always choose to celebrate what we learn, and therefore turn every *failure* into a valuable life lesson. Celebrations don't always have to be our *favorites*, but they can be *favorable*.

Without that daily question, it would be easy for me to miss what's going on in my son's life. And without that question, it would be easy for him to miss it also. The question allows each of us to notice what was wonderful. Attention is given to what he learned. By recalling it, defining it, and articulating it, we further solidify the memory. Sometimes he'll answer my question with, "Nothing happened that was great today." Then I sit there, quietly, and about five seconds later he'll say with a giant smile, "Oh wait ... there *was* something awesome today." I can't tell you how many times I've sat down with my front row journal (you can get a free version of the journal at FrontRowFactor.com/experiment), and asked,

What were my front row moments today?

I just stare at the blank page. My day unfolded literally only hours ago, so why can't I remember what the heck I did during the day? Moments later, the floodgates open, and I start writing. I think to myself, *today was even better than I thought.* It wasn't until later that I learned about a study done by Martin Seligman, the founder of positive psychology, which demonstrated that writing down three good things at the end of each day increases happiness by 2 percent after one week, 5 percent after one month, and 9 percent after six months.[4]

I feel that if I can teach my son to recognize the best moments in life, along with growing from the most challenging ones, he'll develop a powerful mindset that will help him thrive under any conditions. Just as with hope, celebration helps us refocus our attention on those moments in life that give us energy and create a positive distraction from emotional or even physical challenges.

Since our goal with the Front Row Foundation isn't only about helping someone for one day, but changing the way they live every day, forever, we did something unique in the wish-granting world. We opted to celebrate our recipients' experiences, year after year, forever. This allows everyone from the recipient and their family to all staff, donors, and supporters to look back on that moment and feel positive energy, joy, and perhaps some relief from any current challenges they may face.

To celebrate their day, each recipient gets a full-color hardbound book—about 25 pages filled with amazing photographs and commentary—on their front row experience. They also get a professionally edited video documenting their experience. You can view these at FrontRowFoundation. org—and don't forget your tissues.

MEET FRONT ROW RECIPIENT CHRIS CASEY

Chris was a calm and humble guy who was loved by everyone who knew him. He was a husband and father of four outstanding and respectful children. He lit up when asked about his kids, and it was clear that he was an engaged and passionate Dad. Chris was also a sports nut. He and his family were raving fans of their hometown Philadelphia Flyers. The family always watched the games together. After a period of illness during which Chris experienced flu-like symptoms, he learned that he had a baseball-sized tumor inside his chest cavity behind his right shoulder blade. His diagnosis was stage 4 high-grade pleomorphic sarcoma. Since Chris's passion was hockey, the Front Row staff got to work on his event. On the day of his experience, before Chris and his family were escorted to their seats, he was led into a private suite where he was surprised to see a huge group of boys he coached hockey for. They were there to cheer him on and show their support. Chris even got to attend the postgame Press Conference with Flyers head coach Craig Berube.

> See more of Chris' experiences at:
> www.frontrowfoundation.org/chris-casey/

Chris's wife Theresa explained how much they treasured the photo book they received after attending a Philadelphia Flyers game:

We have that on display by our front door, and I show everybody that comes in here. It's the perfect memory of every moment of that wonderful day. The video is my favorite because I don't have a lot of things with Chris's voice on it, and I love listening to his voice and hearing him. That's my absolute favorite. I could sit and listen to it over and over again. It's so nice you created this memory for us, because after someone is gone, that's really what you have to lean on.

————

I knew the pictures and video were important, but I personally underestimated their long-term impact. When our recipients and their families look at their photo book, watch their video, or simply recall the vivid memories etched in their minds, they can relive the magic all over again.

In fact, memories can get better as we get older. According to research conducted by Northwestern Medicine and published in the Journal of Neuroscience[5], the very act of recalling a memory changes it, and often, with repetition, it gets better. Now it's not always *accurate*, but it's better. Reminiscing about positive memories of the past gives us a boost in the present.

These special mementos remind the recipients of their front row experience and help anchor the good feelings repeatedly to pull the past into the present moment.

MEET FRONT ROW RECIPIENT BETH HAHN

Beth was a positive and upbeat woman with a great smile that warmed any heart. Not only was she a devoted wife and a great mother, but she was also extremely passionate about her job as an oncology nurse and organ transplant coordinator. She was a warrior with an amazing heart of gold, willing to share and connect with everyone she met.

Beth's health challenges began in 2004, when she discovered she was faced with a serious diagnosis of ovarian cancer after months of not feeling well. After successfully facing that challenge with surgery and chemotherapy, she was in remission for eight years until, while she was having surgery for a hernia, another tumor was found. Beth had been trying a variety of different therapies in an effort to keep her cancer markers down.

Beth was a raving fan of all things Disney. She and her family are Disney Vacation Club members and have seen

"Beauty and the Beast," as well as some other Broadway shows. Beth's front row experience was a trip to New York to see the Broadway production of "Aladdin." One of the highlights of the performance was when the Genie character began to exit the stage and pointed directly at Beth, just feet from the edge of the stage, and shouted "Beth—I see you out there!" She was witnessed, honored, and celebrated.

> See her story at:
> www.frontrowfoundation.org/beth-hahn/

After the event, weeks had gone by, and one of our team members sent a special gift, which Beth responded to with these words:

Shannon put one of the streamers that were thrown after the show into a little glass bottle and it has been on our kitchen table ever since. Every time we looked at it we're reminded of the day. It's really great because a lot of times we'll sit down to dinner and I haven't taken it off the table. I'll pick it up or Katie will pick it up and we'll talk about … we'll start dinner and we're talking about that day. Remember this, remember that. It's a really good thing to have sitting on our kitchen table, really good thing.

We find fuel for the present moment when we actively choose to celebrate the past and focus on the good.

The best celebrations make people feel witnessed, appreciated, and valued. When we listen deeply and understand someone's values, the best celebrations amplify them. During the writing of this chapter, Beth sadly lost her life. She was loved by everyone in the Front Row family and we will continue to celebrate Beth's life. She will live on forever in our hearts.

A SHIFT IN PERSPECTIVE

In dark moments, it helps to remember the good times. The shift in perspective you get when you remember a positive event from the past can help you deal with the real challenges of the present. Sometimes we forget that we are loved and appreciated. But memories of people showing their affection and support can lift our spirits when we need them most.

We need to feel significant, recognized, and supported, but we also want this for those dear to us. We want their lives to matter. Ella Joy's mother, Anne, talked about how her daughter's most vivid memories from her trip to the front row were of people showing up in the cold to acknowledge and cheer on Ella Joy.

One moment that was really awesome was when we left our house and all our neighbors were there to cheer us on and to see us off in the limo. "I'm a rock star, right? What's happening?" said Ella Joy. That moment really touched my heart because I didn't expect to see that many people there. ... I think it might've even been snowing that day, it was cold. To see people come out, it was really, really a blessing for our family. That's something that the kids constantly go to and they just *want to relive the experience*.

MEET FRONT ROW RECIPIENT MIA GUREVITZ

"Small but mighty" is an accurate description of this little 3-year-old. Several years ago, Mia was diagnosed with a brain tumor (*Pilomyxoid Astrocytoma*) on her pituitary gland, along with spinal lesions of the same tissue type. Mia has gone through life-threatening operations and treatment regimens, but keeps on fighting. Currently her tumor is inoperable and she continues her weekly chemotherapy treatments. Despite all she has been through, she is a happy and smiley little girl.

She adores going to her ballet class, playing with her big sister, doing art projects, and reading books.

Mia's Front Row experience was to attend a performance by her favorite musicians—the famous kids' band called The Fresh Beat Band. She had the time of her life and even got to pose for pictures backstage with the group!

> See more here:
> www.frontrowfoundation.org/mia-gurevitz/

Lisa Gurevitz, Mia's mother, spoke about the power of recalling her front row experience when she said:

From start to finish, from day one when we learned about the Front Row event, we kept saying, "These people are magical!" It was so fun. Mia talks about that day, every day. For almost three years now, it's been the perfect distraction from a time in our lives that was very, very difficult.

We still have these warm-fuzzy feelings about it, and we can relive the day when we look at the photo book. With the video and the pictures, we can scroll back anytime and be back in that moment. It gives us perspective. When you're living with any kind of serious situation, it helps to have that perspective.

MEET FRONT ROW RECIPIENT BRIDGET VALKO

As a wife and mother of three children, Bridget has the reputation of being "the giver" in her family and circle of friends. People who know Bridget will tell you that she is caring, positive, and dependable. The Front Row team would add that she is tenacious, relentless, and *very* funny! In December of 2012, Bridget learned the devastating news that she had stage 2B thymoma cancer (an uncommon cancerous tumor of the thymus), as well as the neuromuscular disorder myasthenia gravis. For Bridget, music has played a large role in helping her to cope with her illnesses and all the treatments. Specifically her favorite singer, Kid Rock, whose concert was of course her front row experience. During the performance, she sang every word to every song. She never sat in her seat once throughout the two-hour performance... a true *raving fan*!

> Check it out:
> www.frontrowfoundation.org/bridget-valko/

Bridget told us this about the photo book we gave her after the show:

My book is out as a coffee-table book. Everyone knows not to set their glass on it, it is not a coaster. It is a book and it constantly reminds me of the event. My happiness that I felt during that. My gratitude from all my friends and my family and the Front Row family of making something that I won't ever forget. My video as well. Getting those captions from my friends, seeing and hearing how much they love me, and to understand what I've conquered and continue to conquer.

In her book *The Happiness Project*, Gretchen Rubin discusses the importance of keeping happy memories vivid. She writes, "As I mulled over this principle, I realized the tremendous value of mementos that help prompt positive memories. Studies show that recalling happy times helps boost happiness in the present. When people reminisce, they focus on positive memories, with the result that recalling the past *amplifies the positive and minimizes the negative.*"[6]

Social psychologist Barbara Fredrickson says that celebration cultivates positive emotions such as joy, gratitude, serenity, interest, hope, pride, amusement, inspiration, awe, and love. We've watched time and time again how our recipients' front row experiences cultivate these same emotions.[7] Through celebration, we can all become moment makers by drawing upon past experiences and bringing power into the present.

HOW WILL YOU CELEBRATE TO AMPLIFY YOUR BEST MOMENTS?

LIVE IN THE MOMENT

Amplify the good, silence what's not.

CHAPTER SEVEN

Facing my own death brought an instant sense of clarity and purpose. If I was indeed going to die, what did I want to say before I went?

—TOM SHADYAC, Film Director

IN CHAPTER 5 WE EXPLORED HOPE. THICH NHAT Hanh, Buddhist monk and peace activist, says, "Hope is important because it can make the present moment less difficult to bear. If we believe that tomorrow will be better, we can bear a hardship today." In chapter 6 we explored celebration.

Oprah Winfrey said, "The more you celebrate your life, the more in life there is to celebrate." Hope and celebration are tools used to bring power to the present moment. This chapter is all about making the most of all those moments you're present for. I've heard that Deepak Chopra wears a watch where instead of telling him the time, it simply displays the word "now." My buddy Rob Scott has tattooed *now* on his arm to remind him of its importance.

The more I worked with people fighting for their lives, the more inspired I became to fight for life itself. I was learning to value more deeply all that I'd been given. I would try to kiss everyone before I walked out the door, not knowing if I'd return. None of us are entitled to another day on this planet. Ultimately, some greater force is calling the shots.

> **Each day is your gift; it's neither earned by you nor owed to you.**

Yes, you can and should eat well, exercise, and avoid risky behavior, but when your time is up, it may be because of something beyond your control. So time is not to be wasted.

On a crisp fall afternoon, my son Tiger and I were hiking the trails not far from our home. After several quiet moments, he turned to me and said, "Papa, I hope you never die. I hope you live for a thousand years."

I said, "I hope I live for a very long time too. Let's make sure to enjoy as much time together as possible."

Tiger, who was five years old at the time, reminded me that these days are special and should not be taken for granted. I often remind myself, *One day, these days will be what we call the good old days.* Although death is certain for us all, living fully in each moment is a choice we must make.

A few days after my son's comment about death, my parents emailed that they were leaving for a long trip overseas. The email read, "In the unlikely event that anything happens to us on our trip, here's where you can find the will."

I felt as if the universe was sending me a message. I took out my journal and put a small dot on the left-hand side of a page and under the dot I wrote *birth*. I drew a line across the page, where I drew another dot. Under that, I wrote *death*. I was 40 years old, and I optimistically assume I'll live a healthy one hundred years, so I put an *X* about where 40 would be—just shy of the halfway point. In front of me was a representation of my entire life on a four-inch line. I could see the whole thing—birth, death, and everything in between—on a single line on a piece of paper.

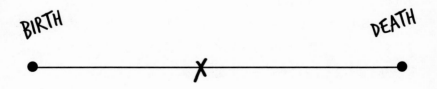

As I looked at the line, I started thinking about how many years I may have left. I know some people run marathons at 90, but no one can truly know their future health, and who knows how long I have. Of course, I'm an optimist and believe I'll experience wellness at the highest level until the day I leave this earth quietly in my sleep at age 100, but I also know that I'm not 100 percent in control of the outcome of this game.

This life timeline exercise was scary. Looking at it on paper I could see an end. And second by second, I was racing against the clock. If I wanted to do something big with my life, I needed to do it now. I also needed to spend time with my family *now*. I needed to write this book *now*. I needed to act with courage and do the thing I was born to do *now*. I also needed to move through my fear so I can live fully *now*.

Dr. Kenneth Vail wrote an article, "When Death Is Good For Life," in which he discussed how the conscious awareness of mortality can motivate people to enhance their physical health and reprioritize intrinsically meaningful goals and values.[8] For me, thinking about my own mortality inspired a new level of vitality in me. When I started questioning where I had been investing my time, with whom, and for what reasons, I got excited thinking about how good some of those decisions were, but I also felt scared because I was spending a good bit of time with people, hanging out in places, and having thoughts that were not serving me.

Today, I'm grateful for a deep awareness of the impermanence of life because it allows me to focus on what's important and make intentional choices based on my values and what's important to me, every day and every moment.

Robin Littman, mother of Front Row recipient Rachel, understands this clearly.

*I had a brother who was five years older than me, and he was tragically killed in an accident. It changed my life, of course, dramatically. It taught me right then and there what life is. It's a **moment**. If we don't take care of that moment, then we're going to get to a place one day where we regret all the moments we didn't live. From that point forward, I believed in living in the present. If I was going to say or do something, I was going to say or do it **now**.*

Palliative care nurse Bronnie Ware wrote a great book called *The Top Five Regrets of the Dying*. She worked for years with people who were near the end of their lives, and over time she noticed a pattern emerging. Her patients commented about having certain regrets about their lives. Here are the five most common:

1. I wish I had the courage to live a life true to myself, not the life others expected of me.
2. I wish I hadn't worked so hard.
3. I wish I'd had the courage to express my feelings.

4. I wish I had stayed in touch with my friends.

5. I wish that I had let myself be happier.

This list stopped me in my tracks, frightened me a bit, and then lit a fire within me with this powerful question: *What has the potential to be the biggest regret at the end of my life?* This powerful question narrows the focus to what we need to do *now* to avoid the kind of regrets we don't want later. What do we need to do *today* to live a life with no regret?

One of my greatest fears is getting to the end of my life and saying:

I wish I had stepped up and shared my voice more courageously in the world and not cared so much about what others think of me.

I wish I had forgiven more quickly so I could freely experience joy instead of pain.

I wish I had accepted the adversities, challenges, and other problems as my greatest assets and not liabilities.

I wish I had focused more on what I do have, and not what's missing.

Considering our final days and hours is powerful because we tend to appreciate the people, experiences, places, and things in our lives only once they are gone.

Front Row recipient Melissa Weaver, who you met earlier in the book, shared with me that before her illness and her Front Row event, she was blind to what was happening in her life. She now says, "I'm going to say yes to things that strengthen me and inspire me."

REFOCUS

Though these life-threatening illnesses tend to bring focus into the present moment, people sometimes talk about how Front Row events distract recipients from their current reality, which might include chemotherapy, radiation, pain, deep discomfort, and their regular routines. Our recipients and their families also talk about how the front row experience interrupts the pattern of everyday life and provides a break. In a sense, it is a distraction. But another way to look at it is as a new focus. A front row moment is a shift in focus.

Distraction is often considered a negative thing, something that keeps us from what's important. Distractions can divert our full attention from our work, for example, but also the pain and discomfort of medical treatments. We provide an opportunity for recipients to shift their focus to the athletes who inspire them, the music they love, and events that allow them to connect with their most authentic selves.

MEET FRONT ROW RECIPIENT TANNER SEABAUM

Tanner had bravely fought serious, life-threatening brain tumors since he was less than two years old. Ultimately, his doctors told his parents that his prognosis was not good, and diagnosed him with a radiation-induced brain stem glioblastoma, which is an inoperable and fatal brain tumor. Despite that, Tanner always lived his life to the fullest, all the while being determined, persistent, and steadfast about his treatments. Tanner's dream event was to attend a Denver Broncos NFL game in his hometown of Denver. Not only was Tanner able to see his beloved Broncos, he also spent time on the field during the pre-game warm ups, and even got to see his two favorite players, Champ Bailey and Peyton Manning, up close. During Tanner's struggles, his parents founded a charity in his name called The Tanner Seebaum Foundation, whose mission is to "positively impact the lives of children with tumors of the brain and spine through funding and supporting viable medical research that will lead to more effective treatment options and ultimately a cure for this tragic disease."

In the *Today Show* story featuring the Front Row Foundation, Matt Seebaum, Tanner's father, said his son was "on a whole different level that day" when he watched the Broncos play. He viewed the game from a seat right behind his favorite players. Tanner's father went on to say, "He was so intent about the game—in the moment all day, and we didn't think once about him being sick or why we were there."

> Read more about Tanner here:
> www.frontrowfoundation.org/tanner-seebaum/

You can't take action in the past or future, only now.

Learning to appreciate where you are gives you the energy and optimism to take actions that bring you closer to your goal. This is at the heart of what my friend Hal Elrod means when he says, "Love the life you have while you create the life of your dreams."

It's okay to notice what's not working in your life. One of my favorite movies, *I AM,* directed by Tom Shadyac, is a film centered around the question *What's wrong with the world and what can we do about it? Noticing* what needs attention, love, and energy often encourages us to grow and improve, connect with our friends and family, and be of service in the world. But *focusing* solely on what's not working to the exclusion of what we can be grateful for robs us of meaning and purpose.

After 11 years of creating these front row experiences, we determined that the essence of a front row life was centered on constantly asking the question *How can we make the most of this moment?* You can find this sentiment echoed through the ages by many brilliant minds. Leo Tolstoy understood this. In his short story "Three Questions," first published in 1885, he revealed the importance of the present moment and the people and circumstances that are in front of you right now.

Remember then: there is only one time that is important—Now! It is the most important time because it is the only time when we have any power. The most necessary man is he with whom you are, for no man knows whether he will ever have dealings with anyone else: and the most important affair is, to do him good, because for that purpose alone was man sent into this life!

Here's how I've personally applied this concept.

What's the best party in town?

The one I'm at.

Who are the best people to be around?

The ones I'm with.

When is the right time?

This very moment.

What kind of life should I be living?

The one I have.

We can find fault with any moment, person, place, or whatever is in front of us. At the same time, with identical scenarios, we can also find what's good if we look for it. So how can we learn to harness the power of hope, celebration, and living in the moment to achieve our wildest dreams and experience life without regret?

That's exactly the question we'll answer in the next 3 chapters. What I'm about to share are the essential ingredients to a life fully lived. I not only came to the conclusion myself, but I've observed with nearly 100 recipients that the minute they choose to focus on the following three ideas, their lives are never the same again.

HOW WILL YOU FULLY ENGAGE IN THE PRESENT MOMENT?

FRONT ROW FOCUS

Focus Determines Feeling

PART THREE

Where focus goes,
energy flows.

—TONY ROBBINS

CULTIVATE AN EMPOWERING MINDSET

What's in your control?

*If you change the way you look at things,
the things you look at change.*

—MAX PLANCK

HAVE YOU EVER BEEN TO A NUDE BEACH? When I walked onto one for the first time, everywhere I looked I saw bronzed bodies frolicking in the waves. The only thing that shocked me was that the average age of those frolicking bodies was 75. *What?* Then it hit me. Maybe when you finally reach that age, you think, *To heck with it. I really don't care if others judge me.*

I thought how powerful it must be to have the mindset that would allow you to be vulnerable, choose joy over fear, and fully accept yourself. These elderly naked beach bums were living life in the front row.

Within the Front Row Foundation, I witness individuals fighting for their lives who accept their current situations and act with courage to overcome adversity and even thrive despite the challenges.

Living life in the front row is a mindset. It's a set of beliefs, values and strategies. It blends the wisdom from our hearts with intellectual design and puts both into motion with bold, courageous action for personal and social impact.

MEET FRONT ROW RECIPIENT NIKKI COLASANTI

Nikki was diagnosed with HER2-positive stage 4 breast cancer and was nominated for a front row experience at a Dallas Cowboys game. Nikki is known to be quick with a joke, loves to laugh, and is a habitual hugger. She loves to read historical mysteries and visit museums, and is both a dog and cat lover. She was born a Texan and has lived many places, but has never stopped rooting for her beloved Cowboys. In December 2016, Nikki attended her Front Row experience at Cowboys Stadium to watch her team play.

> You can see videos and pictures at
> FrontRowFoundation.org/nikki-colasanti

During our limo ride, Nikki said that when she's in public places without a hat, people at times will look at her with disgust. My heart broke. She continued by saying, "It doesn't make me sad, it makes me happy." I was confused until she further explained,

"I'm happy because it means they must not have any context to my situation, which means they couldn't have ever known someone who has battled cancer, and they've certainly never experienced chemotherapy and radiation themselves because if they had, they wouldn't be looking at me that way."

Nikki's mindset is remarkable. Her comment forever changed the way I see the world. Our mindset certainly affects how we experience life emotionally, but could it affect us physically? Researchers today continue to prove just how powerful our mindset is when it comes to impacting our bodies.

In 2007, Harvard researchers Alia Crum and Ellen Langer executed groundbreaking studies to try to understand if the relationship between exercise and health is moderated by one's mindset. In one of these studies,[9] the researchers created a scenario where hotel maids were split into two groups, an experiment group and a control group. The experiment group was told that cleaning was like exercising, the second group did not receive this new information, and both groups went about their regular daily routines. With the knowledge that making beds, scrubbing floors, and picking items up off the floor was just like working out, the informed group actually lost weight in the weeks that followed. The maids who hadn't received any such insight experienced no change. For the members of the experiment group, simply *thinking* that their work was exercise changed the way their bodies responded.

A wide range of studies show that managing our minds is critical to our overall well-being. Learning to influence our thoughts, beliefs, values, perceptions, attitudes, and emotions is essential to living life in the front row. It's our mindset that matters most. When someone is battling an illness trying to take over their body, their mindset is a critical factor in the healing process. I'm not a doctor and don't believe you can wish away cancer, but I do believe we're only scratching the surface in understanding the power of the mind. I would confidently argue that positive thinking, along with good energy, prayers, and love from those around us, can positively influence our health.

In 2012, the University of Wisconsin School of Medicine and Public Health conducted a study that Stanford University psychologist Kelly McGonigal quoted in her TED talk "How To Make Stress Your Friend."[10] The study tracked 30,000 adults for eight years. They asked participants about how much stress they experienced and if they believed stress was bad for their health. People who experienced a lot of stress had a 43 percent increased risk of dying, but that was only true for people who *believed* that stress is harmful for their health. People who experienced a lot of stress but believed it wasn't harmful had the lowest chance of dying of anyone in the study, even compared to those who experienced very little stress. The researchers estimated that during the eight years the study was going on, 182,000 Americans died not from stress, but from the belief that stress is bad for you. If that estimate is true, then believing stress is bad for you is the 15th largest cause of death in the U.S.

We can learn to shift our mindset. We can learn to see stress as our friend. We can reprogram and recondition the mind. What would you be capable of by fully accessing the power of your mind? How would it affect you emotionally, physically, or in any other aspect of life? What if we knew exactly how to use our imagination to influence our reality in ways that allow us to fend off fear and continually step up with courage? At the end of your life, what might you experience if you made even more bold moves toward your highest aspirations? I've noticed how a powerful mindset in our recipients has been the most critical factor in the quality of their lives.

I've found that there are two main beliefs that make up a front row mindset:

1. **The belief that we must fully accept and embrace the parts of our reality we can't change**

2. **The belief that we create the future we want through taking bold actions today**

But how do we know when to set a new standard, step up, and no longer accept our current situation versus being grateful for what we have while in pursuit of what we want? Welcome to the art of moment making.

THE BEST SEAT

I think many of us, at times, wish we had someone else's seat. Several weeks ago, I was at a Philadelphia Phillies baseball game. When I was buying tickets, I asked for the best seats in the house. The woman at the ticket window said, I have row 7 for $70, but I have to tell you, they're in the sun and it's going to be blazing hot today. I also have row 27 for $35, and they're in the shade. I opted for shade—being kind to my bald head and wallet. About 45 minutes into the game, several guys who were sitting somewhere near row 7 moved back closer to our seats and said, "It's too damn hot down there." I was reminded that sometimes the best seats are the ones you've got. Most of us are really in pursuit of a *front row experience*, not always necessarily the front row itself.

LIFE IS ABOUT FINDING *YOUR* FRONT ROW.

We have a saying in our house with our boys—you get what you get and you don't get upset. At times, we don't choose our seats, and moving isn't an option, and this is where fully accepting your reality and enjoying what you have is key. It's important to free yourself of envy and jealousy, as they rob you of the joy felt through appreciation. I've noticed that when I'm not in the business of comparing myself to others or wishing I were somewhere else, it dawns on me that I'm really, really happy.

If you ever start to feel anxious about your current seat in life, perhaps consider there is a reason you've got the seat you do and it's up to you to find out why.

Could it teach you something?

Could your seat offer a perspective you wouldn't have had in any other seat?

Could there be a person sitting nearby you're destined to meet?

Even if you're not fighting a life-threatening illness, we've all played victim and gotten wrapped up into how things "should" be. We struggle when our expectations don't meet our reality. Instead of "This is how it should have been in my life," try saying "Okay, this is where I'm at, and so I'm going to do the best I can with what I've got." This isn't settling, this is strategy.

Jennifer Lay, the mother of Logan who we introduced to you earlier in chapter 5, said:

This experience put us back on the right track and helped us to realize that life is amazing and that although it's not exactly the picture that we had painted, it is what we have and we really want to make the most of it. We don't want to have any regrets, we don't want to spend any more time feeling sadness and loss for what isn't. We want to focus on what we do have and what is and what's possible. This whole year has felt like it's been a complete shift in all of our mindsets. I think I can attribute a lot of that to having such a cool event to kick off the year. Although we were going to see such a high-profile celebrity, we were made to feel that we were the high-profile celebrity.

LEARN AND LET GO

It's hard for someone to have a front row mindset and be a moment maker when they're living in the past. Being fully present now includes letting go and disengaging from the limiting beliefs and negative stories we've held onto about our past. Just because you've been a back row person all your life doesn't mean that has to continue. Tony Robbins says, "Your biography is not your destiny." Moving to the front row means letting go of the back. Celebrating now is hard to do when we're hung up on something negative. A guest on the Oprah Winfrey show once said this about forgiveness, "It really means letting go of the past we thought we wanted," and of course, the past is anything that occurred already, including something just moments ago. He also said "Forgiveness is giving up the hope that the past could be any different."[11]

This morning, as I write this, I got hung up on an argument my wife and I had last night. I woke up this morning to work on the book and felt paralyzed with negative emotions. I realized that, to move forward, I needed to let go of my anger. I called her and said, "I love you. When we fight, I don't function well. Let's start over." We made up quickly, and it was done. I was off to writing again.

I have some very successful friends whose lives could appear perfect from the outside, but they make just as many mistakes as anyone. I have a front row seat to their lives and at times see their challenges up close and personal. I've often asked, what makes them so successful when they fail so often? My buddy John Kane says it best, **"Just learn the lesson and forget the details."** Whether you call this forgetting the details, forgiveness, letting go, or moving on— it's all about shifting our paradigm off of *what was* to *what could be.*

Who do you need to forgive today?

What do you need to let go of?

Who would you be if you chose to shed all your limiting beliefs?

How would you feel if you released the negative feelings you're currently holding on to about yourself and others?

Years ago, my amazing coach and friend, Fi Mazanke, advised me to write a letter to someone I'd been very angry with. Under her advisement, I wrote it, then burned it and let it go forever. It was an incredibly powerful exercise and created an immediate emotional shift for me. I felt instantly lighter. Often, we miss opportunities to be moment makers now, because we're too hung up on something that's already long gone.

PERFECTION

My buddy Jon Berghoff often says, "It's perfect"—especially in challenging situations that most would see as nowhere near perfect. When he says *It's perfect*, he's not necessarily saying *It's preferred*. If it were within his control, he might have chosen a different situation. If you can't choose a different situation, for example if you're stuck in traffic, Jon would respond, "Oh, this is perfect ... this is a great chance to think, make a few phone calls, or just practice being patient." Why waste energy fighting things that you can't change?

When my buddy Hal Elrod gets upset, he allows himself five minutes to be angry, and then he says, "Can't change it" and moves on. I've seen him do this in less than five seconds for some pretty challenging stuff.

Shawn Achor says,

"Happiness is not about lying to ourselves, or turning a blind eye to the negative, but about adjusting our brain so that we see the ways to rise above our circumstances."[12]

Perhaps the next time you face a seemingly less than perfect scenario, you can remind yourself that within every situation, favorable or not, there is a lesson and opportunity if you choose to see it. How can you reconnect and engage your senses fully in the present moment? My mindfulness coach Julianna Raye says, "We imagine this or that desire will lead us to fulfillment. Mindfulness helps us find it in each moment." Julianna has given me the gift of a daily mindfulness practice.

> **Take a moment, pause for 60 seconds, breathe deep, with your eyes open, and ask yourself three questions:**
>
> **1. What do you see?**
>
> **2. What do you hear?**
>
> **3. What do you feel?**

Did you notice things happening in the background that previously went unnoticed? The hum of the fan, a breeze on your face, or the sound of your own breath. There is often so much happening around us that we are able to tune out. This is neither good nor bad. Julianna says, "The key is to have choice, so that when you would like to narrow your focus in order to move forward you can do that skillfully and when you would like to open up and discover the options you can do that skillfully as well." By developing skillful attention you become a better moment maker.

It isn't enough just to pay attention—the way you focus is key. It takes practice, but once you understand how to fully appreciate any moment, all moments have the power to transform. When you let yourself be transformed, moment making happens.

Years ago, I hosted a large fundraiser in Philadelphia. My buddy John Kane walked up to me and said, "Hey man, take a quick moment and look around. Soak it in. All these people love you and are here to support Front Row. This is a great moment. Forget the details of running the event and take a second to *be* at your event. Feel the love in this room and let that energize you." John is a moment maker. He's done stuff like this all the time. He's able to see the brilliance in any situation. He's mindful enough to notice what's needed in the moment and has the courage to act on it.

Jon Kabat-Zinn, the founder of Mindfulness Based Stress Reduction says, "Mindfulness is awareness that arises through paying attention, on purpose, in the present moment, non-judgmentally, in the service of self understanding and wisdom."[13]

ACT WITH COURAGE

A huge part of living a front row life is knowing *what* show *you* want to see. In fact, it's the genesis of a front row experience when we find out what live event the recipient would most want to see. We want to know what makes them feel most alive. Isn't that the quintessential question—**what makes us come alive?**

Around ninth grade, I *loved* blues and jazz. That is, until someone told me it wasn't *cool* and I should listen to something else. My need to connect overpowered my need for blues and jazz, so I just conformed to whatever was popular. It wasn't until years later that my neighbor Ernie handed me a disc and said, "This is awesome music. Check it out."

He had handwritten in sharpie: *Pink Martini: Hang On Little Tomato.* I would soon find out the band was made up of 12 members who play a blend of classical music and jazz with a little old-fashioned pop. *I LOVED IT!* I came alive! This gift was monumental for me. Ernie would learn later that by handing me that disc, he became a moment maker. A great part of my adult life has been peeling away the layers to find my true self. One of the most valuable lessons I've learned over the years is that personal growth doesn't have to be about learning something new. It can simply be remembering something true.

PURSUE YOUR MUSIC NOW

When I think of recipients with extraordinary mindset, I think of Tanner, who you met earlier. His father Matt told me that when the doctors found the tumor, they told Tanner,

"If there's something you want to do, go do it right now."

To which Tanner replied, "It's time to get busy living." Battling the real and raw emotions, they still found the strength to consciously choose to make each day count.

Tanner was into electronic dance music, so his parents signed him up for some DJ lessons. He loved it and his talents progressed quickly. Very soon he was even able to DJ at a big event in Las Vegas and when he took the stage, he was in his element. There was even a documentary, *Beat 4 Tanner*, that was made about his life.

Beth Hahn, a recipient you also heard from earlier, said this:

We try to do as much as we can so that when people say to me, 'Oh I always wanted to do that,' my answer is always, 'Well do it. What's keeping you from doing it? Just get on the internet and book it.' There are things that I really want to do before I'm too sick, and you just have to do it. I don't know if we're going to get a tomorrow. I always say I could die in a car accident on the way to my treatment. Yeah you need to live a Front Row life, because this is the only one.

QUESTIONS MAKE THE MOMENT

One way to cultivate a powerful mindset is to ask intentional questions. When we ask questions, the brain can't help but look for answers. Questions determine thoughts, thoughts influence action, actions repeated become habits, and habits determine results. So everything begins with the right question. Voltaire says "Judge a man by his questions rather than his answers."

Making the moment begins with making the question.

THE BEST QUESTION

My buddy Jon was in a meeting when one of the executives of the company placed a $100 gift card on the table and stated, "This is a prize, not for the best idea today, but for the best question."

Questions offer possibility; answers offer clarity. Both are important and certainly have their place. Just like any tool, we need to know when to use them.

Living a front row life might mean asking, "How can I enjoy my current seat even more right now?" Other times it's "How can I get a better seat?" or maybe it's not as much about you as it is those around you, "How can I help others have an even better experience?" Questions create focus, focus creates feelings, and feelings make up our emotional experience of life.

During one-on-one coaching sessions with my private clients, I want to make sure we're asking the right question. I'll typically lead with *What's the question we most want to answer today?* Then, I often question the question. I'll ask *Is this the question you really want an answer to? Is this the most important question to answer when it comes to living out your #1 goal or dream right now?* Half the time, it's not. So we design a new question and move from there.

During my interviews for the *Front Row Factor* podcast, my goal is to ask questions that inspire my guest to say, "That's an awesome question" or "I've never been asked that before." As I prepare for every interview, I know I'm a moment maker for three groups of people:

First, it's a powerful moment for me. I'm learning so much from each guest. When I ask my guest a question, even though I'm focused on what my guest is saying, my subconscious is processing the same question.

Next, it's a powerful moment for our listeners. The questions for my guests become listener questions. Listeners not only benefit from asking the questions themselves, but they get the perspective of my guests' answers.

Third, it's powerful for my guests. When I ask them a question, I give them the chance to articulate what's important once again. They likely refine their answers even if they've given them many times before. It's an affirmation along with an exploration.

Questions are a powerful force for good, and are the genesis for a front row life.

In a brief yet powerful conversation I had with the great Kevin Spacey, he shared with me his secret to a great life. He said *Be curious*. What would today look like if you brought a childlike wonder to each and every moment? The good news for you is that you were once a kid with a wide-eyed and endless curiosity and you can access it anytime you like. A moment maker is open to possibilities. They ask: What is great about now? What resources exist that we can use to make this moment special? What would make this moment one we'll talk about for years to come? Who can we serve right now? Who else can we involve in this experience? Curiosity is key.

When we host front row experiences, I've found that asking great questions can create an awesome experience. For example, I remember sitting around the table with half a dozen people, and I asked everyone to play a game. I suggested we all go around the table and say one thing we love about the recipient. After the first person shared, there were tears. It was not only powerful for the recipient to hear such beautiful things, but it was powerful for those who got a chance to say them and see the response. Everyone had a memory for life. Moment makers ask great questions.

THREE QUESTIONS

I challenge you, during conversations in the next 24 hours, to ask three questions before commenting. So many times we want to chime in with our own stories and solutions. This challenge is harder than it first appears. When you ask someone what they're doing, they may reply with something like, "I'm running my first marathon," and you're tempted to reply, "So awesome. I ran a marathon last year and it was a great experience." While I understand you're trying to relate and connect, hold back from turning the attention to you, keep the spotlight on them, and roll with more questions. "Do you have a goal to finish in a certain time? How will you celebrate when it's all over? Are you running with anyone else? How long have you been training for this? Do you have a specific run strategy for the day?"

From coaching conversations to casual chitchats, it's very hard (I fail often here) for me to not offer up commentary with immediate solutions, tools, or resources that I know will help. Oftentimes, I'll chime in just before that person has the chance to reveal something super important. I remind myself regularly to just ask another question and remain curious.

MORNING QUESTIONS

Since questions create focus, I needed to find a way to ask the best questions each morning to direct my attention. To be a moment maker each day, I need to prime my mind to be looking for opportunities. I printed the following questions and put them near my reading chair, hung them in the bathroom, and put them next to my computer. I don't read every question every day, but nine days out of ten, the first two questions are at the top of my mind. The questions are always evolving as my life does. Here are a few of my favorites:

1. How will I be a moment maker today?

2. What is the one thing I must focus on today that will have the biggest impact on my life and the lives of others?

3. Where must I say NO to the people, places, or things that are distracting me from my highest priorities?

4. How can I be the best dad and husband today?

5. How can I connect with, recognize, thank, and/or add value to my most important relationships (a.k.a. my front row)?

6. What am I doing to create systems that can function without me, so that we will impact the world for decades to come?

7. What am I grateful for right now? (People, resources, opportunities, etc.)

8. What's the best thing that can happen today?

EVENING QUESTIONS

At night, I'll often ask several questions to wrap up the day. I write them in my front row journal. Questions 1 and 2 are ones I ask nightly. Questions 3 through 8 I ask weekly. At dinner each night, I ask my kids about their front row moments and failures. The very activity of asking for their front row moments often becomes *my* front row moment.

1. What front row moments can I celebrate today?

2. Where did I fall/fail and what can I learn from it?

3. What was better today than yesterday?

4. What am I grateful for?

5. What dream makes me feel most alive, and what's the next step to fulfill it?

6. What is the most important question I need to answer right now?

7. In what ways did my environment help or hinder me and what's one adjustment I can make for tomorrow?

8. Of my top eight relationships, whose dream can I support right now and how?

In 2016, we invited about 30 individuals from the Front Row Community to a special gathering we call *The Front Row Summit*, which is designed to facilitate conversation around the future of the Front Row Foundation. There were board and staff members, donors, recipients, and other fans of the front row. During that meeting, we asked everyone to define their front row moments in life and what qualities made up those moments. We were attempting to define the mindset of someone who lives life in the front row. Through hours of exploration and collaboration, the group landed on four main ideas, which most simply stated are: Presence, Courage, Community, and Transformation. How would your days be different if you more consistently asked:

1. How can I be fully present in this moment?

2. How can I act with courage in this moment?

3. How can I connect and build community in this moment?

4. How can I create a transformative experience for myself and others?

LIVING LIFE IN THE FRONT ROW IS A PRACTICE

Just like anything, without focus and attention, performance fades. If I'm not careful, my old back row mindset returns to haunt me. Old unhealthy habits can be hard to break, but breaking them is a must. Being in the front row requires courage. There's no doubt a certain level of accountability and vulnerability there, too—for some more than others. With your back to the crowd and eyes forward, you're now a leader not a follower. The front row isn't always easy. In fact, it can be super crowded and uncomfortable at times, yet vulnerability and certain inconveniences are part of chasing your dreams. It's not supposed to be easy, it's supposed to be meaningful.

What perspective most empowers me in this moment?

CULTIVATE EMPOWERING RELATIONSHIPS

Who will you stand for?

CHAPTER NINE

The only way to have a friend is to be one.

—RALPH WALDO EMERSON

ON A BEAUTIFUL SUNNY AFTERNOON AT THE PARK with my son Tiger, the usual monkey bars and slides had been taken over by a giant inflatable bounce house, roller coaster, and 40-foot rock-climbing wall. Tiger, who was four at the time, asked if he could climb the wall. I remember thinking, *there's no way he can do it. This is for the big kids.*

I encouraged him to try something geared toward kids his age. "Hey buddy, let's ride the roller coaster. You love that!"

He wouldn't bite and was persistent in his quest to climb the wall.

I said, "All right, let's give it a shot," but inside I was thinking, *there's no way he's going to be able to do this. He's just not big enough.*

Minutes later Tiger had his harness on and was ready to rock. Without hesitation, he grabbed the wall and, looking like he'd done this 100 times before, effortlessly shot toward the top. *What?! I'm blown away!* About 30 feet up the wall he stopped. He had reached a part of the wall that was inverted. *This part is for the pros,* I remember thinking, *there's no way he's making it past this.* I was right.

In that moment, he turned around, gazed down at me with defeated eyes, and shouted, "Papa, I can't."

I looked up at him and shouted words of consolation, "It's okay buddy, you tried." Inside I thought, *I knew that was too difficult.*

Before Tiger could give up and rappel down, the attendant turned to me and said, "I think your boy can do it." He looked up to my son and said,

"Hey buddy, try again!"

My boy grabbed the wall with his newfound confidence, and with every ounce of energy he could muster within his tiny, 35-pound body, he focused, struggled, and eventually reached the top. Everyone started cheering. He did it!

I was shocked.

What happened there? How is it possible that the guy working the rock wall believed in my son more than I had?

The answer is quite simple and far too common.

People often treat others as they remember them from yesterday, not as who they are today or who they could become at any given moment. We project our own limiting beliefs on others. This happens all the time—for parents, couples, managers, or leaders, and even between friends. The guy working the rock wall didn't know my son prior to that moment, so he didn't bring any limiting beliefs to the situation, and therefore only projected potential. Since that day, I've been more conscious in the way I show up as a father for Tiger. I suppose I also get to "try again."

That man was a moment maker for my son. I'm guessing that to this day he doesn't know the power behind his words in that moment, "Hey buddy, try again," and how they forever impacted my family's life. It's interesting to think how many times in your life, you've been a moment maker for someone else and not known it. It's also fun to think about how many times you can be a moment maker in the days ahead.

> ## Today, be a fan.
>
> ## Lift others up.
>
> ## Be in their front row.

Imagine band members playing their hearts out for the crowd. They light up when they see someone singing along, dancing, and being totally caught up in the moment. You, as a fan, feed the band with positive energy, and in turn the band feeds you. **Fans who give energy get a better show.**

During a podcast interview with Niyi Sobo, a former running back for the New Orleans Saints, he told me, "In my first game, I remember I started against the 49ers. I caught my first pass, and I ran and got tackled by this guy. And then I heard the whole stadium just erupt. It was like an eight or nine yard catch. And it was in that moment, that I was like, shoot, I almost forgot I was playing pro ball." I then asked, "How important are the fans?" He said, "Fans are the positive reinforcement. The environment is very important." On some days you'll be a fan, and on other days you'll feel the love from your fans.

I try to enter each new relationship asking, *What would it look like to be their biggest fan?* Kevin Kelly wrote a popular essay entitled "1,000 True Fans."[14] He defines a true fan as "a fan that will buy anything you produce." The concept was for "anyone making things, or making things happen." He explains, "To make a living as a craftsperson, photographer, musician, designer, author, animator, app maker, entrepreneur, or inventor you need only thousands of true fans." What would change in your world if you had 1,000 true fans? How can you first treat others like rockstars and be their #1 fan? Just remember that, to have fans, you must be one. You step up for others and add value, and they'll likely do the same. If you want fans in your front row, make sure to show up for them first. Aside from simply being the right thing to do, I also know that when I stand, cheer, and show appreciation and respect, I'll get a better performance. Everyone wins.

THE BUSINESS OF MOMENT MAKING

One of the best moment makers I know is my friend John Ruhlin, the author of the book *Giftology*. John is a master of relationship building. He has an uncanny ability to make people feel like rockstars. He takes a bold approach to building front row relationships in his life and business. Here is one of my favorite examples.

John had identified Cameron Herold as someone he wanted to connect with. Cameron had built two $100 million dollar companies, including 1-800-GOTJUNK? These days, he's a business coach to some of the world's most prominent CEOs.

In a brief conversation, John learned that Cameron was a fan of Brooks Brothers, a high-end men's clothing store. When he learned that Cameron would be in the area, he arranged to meet up. He then picked out $7,000 worth of clothing in Cameron's size—shirts, suits, you name it—and turned Cameron's hotel room into a Brooks Brothers store. John treated Cameron to a shopping spree inside his hotel room, and in the process created an unforgettable front row moment. Cameron was blown away. He told John, "Whatever you want to talk about for as long as you want to talk about it, I'm all ears." Because John is a moment maker, he has thousands of true fans. Having a thousand raving fans doesn't happen overnight, but rather one moment, one connection at a time.

Creating fans also doesn't require loads of money, time, or energy. Sometimes the best moments are simple, spontaneous, and free. For example, my buddy Jeff Kaylor is an incredible performer whose signature keynote presentation *Creating Magic Moments* combines brilliant magic to teach essential life and business skills. One of the stories he shares is how a simple piece of rubber shrimp has helped him meet incredible people, including acquiring new clients. Imagine you're with Jeff out for breakfast and he orders oatmeal. When the server delivers the food, just before they walk away, he sneaks the shrimp onto the food and calls out, "Excuse me, but was my oatmeal supposed to come with shrimp?" The server is utterly confused. Jeff lets the confusion really set in, and finally reveals the prank. Everyone laughs. He's made countless friends by bringing joy to what would have been an ordinary moment for not only the server, but everyone at the table, and often the tables around them who are simply caught up in the laughter.

I loved the rubber shrimp idea so much, I tried this out for myself one morning at breakfast. I shoved the shrimp into the end of my omelet. Keep in mind there's not a single item with shrimp on the menu. When I asked the server about the shrimp, she just stared without blinking trying to figure out what happened. When I finally gave in and told her, she couldn't stop laughing. I thought the joke was over. At the end of the meal when I went to pay, she told me my credit card was declined. I gave her another card. She came back a few minutes later and told me the second one was declined. I didn't have cash or any more credit cards, so after making me sweat for a second, she started laughing, and told me my cards were fine, she was just getting me back! Everyone at the table laughed. We took a group picture with the waitress. It was a front row moment all because of a rubber shrimp.

MOMENT MAKING MOMENTUM

What's fun about giving the gift of a front row moment is that it starts a ripple. When one person holds the door for another, perhaps it starts a chain reaction for many others. Recipient Melissa Weaver brings this point home with these comments about the power of being given a photo book of her Front Row experience.

When I saw the photo book of our Front Row celebration at the Sarah McLachlan concert, I thought, *Oh, I want to feel that again. I want to feel that level of inspiration again.* And I thought, *How am I going to do that? How am I going to get back to this place?*

That's when I decided,

I know how. I'm going to start giving back, because that way someone else will get that feeling, so that feeling lives on in someone else.

Because I was so transformed by the experience, it's become more than a day for me. It's become a way of living. I guess when I talk to people about it, that's what I say, is that this day has turned into a way of life.

MEET FRONT ROW RECIPIENT
SOPHIE JANE DARR

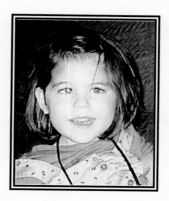

I'll never forget when we received a request for a little 4-year-old girl, Sophie, who was a raving fan of Kelly Clarkson. Our team created a magical day with a limo ride, dinner at the Rainforest Cafe, and then off to the show. The most magical part of the night came after the show, when Sophie was fast asleep in her mother's arms. We surprised her with a private meeting with Kelly.

Lauren Clapper, Sophie's mom, said, "That was the best day of my life with her. The Front Row Foundation created that for us. They didn't even know us. Just how far they went to make her happy is amazing to me, and they continue to be family to me."

Sadly, Sophie lost her battle with her brain tumor shortly after this event. Everyone's heart was broken. Today I get very emotional just thinking about Sophie and her amazing smile. I keep a photograph of the moment when Sophie met Kelly in my office. The picture of Sophie's front row moment continues to remind me of the importance of our mission. To bring this full circle, John Ruhlin was the one who had the relationship that got Sophie backstage and the one who gave me the framed photo I now treasure.

AROUND THE WORLD IN 24 HOURS

A common question we get at the Front Row Foundation is "How do you get the tickets for Front Row events?" Ninety percent of the time, it's through the generosity of the people in our network. A friend or a friend of a friend. Relationships are the key that unlocks almost any door. Here's the perfect example.

MEET FRONT ROW RECIPIENT JAIDEN TAYLOR

Jaiden was a young boy who loved NASCAR. Diagnosed with stage 4 neuroblastoma cancer as a five-year-old, Jaiden has endured more than his share of treatments. Though these treatments battle the cancer, they often leave him feeling too sick and tired to play. On his worst days of chemotherapy reactions, only one thing could lift his spirits, and that was NASCAR. As sick as he was, he would always watch his favorite racer, Jeff Gordon. Many times when Jaiden was hospitalized, he would watch the races from his hospital bed, cheering Gordon on to victory.

Our team wanted desperately to create a front row experience for Jaiden, so we went on the hunt for tickets to the next NASCAR event. I posted on Facebook, "Need help for a five-year-old boy battling cancer. Looking for tickets to NASCAR and maybe a connection to Jeff Gordon."

Within minutes of posting the message, my friend Kris Mailepors, who was getting his MBA in New Zealand, saw the post and jumped into action by sharing the request on a NASCAR bloggers page. The vice president of a big company that works with NASCAR saw the post and sent me an email. "We heard about your quest for tickets for Jaiden. We'd like to help. Where can we overnight them?"

But that's not where the story ends.

Another friend, Marcus Holman, also saw my post. He texted his buddy Bill Gooch, who knows Gordon personally. A couple of text messages later, Jaiden was scheduled to meet Jeff Gordon himself at his trailer before the race!

What?!

Are you kidding me?

Within 24 hours, a small group of giving friends with powerful relationships made magic happen for Jaiden. When I look back over the past ten years, we have found tickets for the vast majority of our Front Row experiences because of powerful connections.

In the book *Connected: The Surprising Power of Our Social Networks*, authors James H. Fowler and Nicholas A. Christakis share compelling evidence that we can profoundly influence and be influenced by the people in our lives. We affect one another's health, wealth, and happiness. Fowler and Christakis say, "Social networks do things that no single person can do." To me, Jaiden's story is a perfect example of that. And I'm always amazed that, when it counts most, people step up.

YOUR FRONT ROW

Imagine life is like a concert, and you're on stage. Who do you want in your front row? You likely have many friends, but you can share only a limited number of front and center seats. Knowing who those people are is a critical factor in living life in the front row.

Let's play a game for a minute. Read these questions and think of the first people that pop up.

1. Who am I with when I laugh the most?

2. Who am I with when I learn the most?

3. Who am I with when I feel most alive?

4. Who shows up in my darkest hours?

5. Who do I call when I'm proud and want to celebrate?

6. Who do I think of when I say "amazing friend"?

7. Who asks me about my dreams and goals?

8. Who brings out the best in me?

> I want people in my front row who make me come alive. I want those whose energy inspires me to be the best version of myself. Each year, I sit down in a coffee shop and ask myself, Who's in my front row? I'm looking for eight names. Choosing someone to be in your top eight means that others won't be. I want to be best friends with everyone, but it's just not possible. I can know thousands and care for many, but my front row is different—it's limited to eight.

When we select a recipient for a front row experience, we try to get as many tickets as possible, but that's often a limited number. The recipient needs to choose who they want to share that experience with. Your life is similar in that each day you make choices, consciously or not, about who you invest your time with. Who in your life should be in your front row?

The Front Row Foundation was built by people wanting to help others live out their biggest dreams. In the book *The Dream Manager*, Matthew Kelly poses the question, *"Isn't one of our primary responsibilities of all relationships to help each other fulfill our dreams?"* If you're a business owner or leader of teams, his book points out that helping your employees live out their personal dreams helps people engage more deeply in their work.

When I interview people for my podcast, my goal is to create a high-quality connection with my guest. A high-quality connection is an interaction that makes each party feel engaged, open, motivated, and revitalized.[15] In order for me to feel the connection, I must be learning about my guest and their dreams. I believe that lifting others up, celebrating them, honoring them, and focusing on helping them feel fulfilled are some of the most fulfilling things we can do.

When I make my list of Top 8, I write next to each name what dream makes them come alive. I hang this list next to my desk, and I see it daily. I'll often send a text message randomly with something like this, "*Hey, what are you doing today to get closer to your big dream this year?* Zig Ziglar was quoted as saying, "You will get all you want in life, if you help enough other people get what they want." Henry David Thoreau said, "Friends ... they cherish one another's hopes. They are kind to one another's dreams."

Nobody knows better the power of having quality relationships than those who are fighting for their lives. It's wonderful to have friends around when things are great, it's critical to have friends when things aren't.

A PERFECT MATCH

I love thinking that, on any given day, I may meet someone who becomes one of the most important people in my life.

In my early thirties, I had one of those days. As a single guy who worked hard, I was looking for ways to earn extra money while meeting some new friends. So I decided to get a roommate. Sifting through applications, I answered the request from a woman named Tatyana who wanted to stop by and see my place. On the drive over, she called and said, "I'm trying to get to you, but I'm lost."

She told me where she was, and I replied,

> "No problem. I know exactly where you are. Just turn left onto Erial Road and then turn right on Hickstown Road."
>
> While on the phone with me, she said, "Great, got it, done."
>
> I said, "Now, take your first right, and you should see my neighborhood."
>
> She said, "I'm back at the gas station."
>
> I laughed. "What! How is that possible!? Let's try again. Pull out of the gas station, then turn left."
>
> She responded, "Done."

I said, "Go to the next traffic light. It's Hickstown Road. Turn right."

Again, she replied, "Okay, done."

I said, "Now go to the next street and turn right."

Confidently she said again, "Done."

I asked, "Where are you?"

She said, "Back at the gas station."

I'm laughing hysterically. "How is that even possible?"

If I were to draw this on a map for you, it'd actually make sense. The gas station has two exits and, to add to the confusion, two of those roads share a name.

I told her to stay put while I hopped in my car and drove out to meet her. After I parked, we both stepped out of our cars at the same time. I still remember that moment like it was yesterday. I saw a gorgeous smile that lit up my world instantly. While my heart said, "Wow! Who is this girl?" my mind said, "Oh boy, I'm in trouble!" I managed to keep my jaw from hitting the ground. Outside I was playing it cool, but inside, I was melting.

We hit it off instantly. If she was really going to move into my home, I wanted to have an honest conversation about lifestyle, needs, values, and other important stuff. I suggested we sit down for a beer and get to know each other. I know that living with someone is a big commitment, and I wanted to make sure we would get along.

As we sipped our drinks, we shared stories, asked questions, and talked honestly. We hit it off, and it wasn't long after she decided to move in that I invited her to go see a live band in Old City Philadelphia. We talked and laughed endlessly. It was a perfect night. I noticed that when the show began, we got closer to one another. We were acting less and less like roommates having a night out and more and more like this was our first date.

The night ended with our first kiss. It didn't escape me throughout this entire experience that dating your roommate has disaster written all over it. Thankfully, my roommate was my soulmate.

We spent every moment possible together. It all happened so fast. The next minute we were Christmas-tree shopping with our friends John and Tracy Kane. As I loaded the tree, John happened to see Tatyana talking with a little girl who was selling hot chocolate. John watched Tatyana give the little girl a $5.00 bill and tell her to keep the change.

I knew that at that time Tatyana certainly didn't have any excess cash. She was working two jobs to pay the bills, and every dollar counted. Tatyana didn't know that John had seen this whole thing go down, but later, when John pulled me aside and told me the story, he said, *"In that moment*, I saw her heart. I see why you love her. You can learn a lot about someone by how they act when nobody is watching." Little did Tatyana know that her $5 "keep the change" moment was important for our relationship. Her actions influenced John, and John's comment influenced me.

One year after Tatyana moved in as my roommate, I proposed, and six months after that, we were married in her hometown of Krasnoyarsk, Siberia.

People ask me today, "How did you know she was the one?" The answer, "You'll know when you don't have to ask that question."

Learning to listen to our hearts, especially with relationships, is one of the most important skills to develop.

> **When I wake up each day, I think that one of the most important relationships of my life is out there, and I may have the opportunity to meet them.**

GIVE AND TAKE

Being in the front row is about giving first. But in order for someone to give big, there must be someone willing to receive. Being a great gift *getter* is as important as being a great gift *giver*. When we're open to receiving, we allow others the joy of giving.

I once gave a keynote presentation, and afterwards a woman said, "That was awesome. That's exactly what I needed to hear. You are the best speaker ever."

I thought the correct response was to show humility. "I don't know about *best speaker ever*, but thank you very much." I quickly realized that, although my comment was intended to be kind and humble, I was ultimately rejecting her comment.

If she believes I'm the best speaker ever, who am I to tell her she's wrong? She's entitled to her opinion and belief. Today when someone shares kind words with me, I respond, "Thank you so much. I'm so happy you enjoyed it. What part did you like the most?" I put my ego in check and realize the gift isn't about me. It's about honoring the giver. Receiving gifts is often hard for people. We see this show up at the Front Row Foundation.

Theresa's husband, Chris Casey, celebrated Front Row-style at a Philadelphia Flyers game with his family and many of the children he coached in hockey. Here is what she had to say about Chris accepting his Front Row Experience:

I was so happy that he was open and willing to do this, willing to be part of the Front Row event, because he was not a 'center of attention' kind of guy. He was always ... he kept to himself, and he was always involved in things and worked really hard and volunteered at things, but he never wanted the glory. I found myself after he passed even more grateful that we all had that opportunity and that time and that incredible memory.

———

Even though Chris didn't love the spotlight, he allowed it so that his wife, his children, and the children he coached could have this wonderful experience to live on after he passed. He showed love by accepting love—a truly generous act.

Where do you need to be more accepting of the gifts that others want to send your way? The most selfless thing to do is accept with gratitude and then find ways to pay it forward. The cycle continues, and momentum builds.

Chris gave his family a true gift by accepting one.

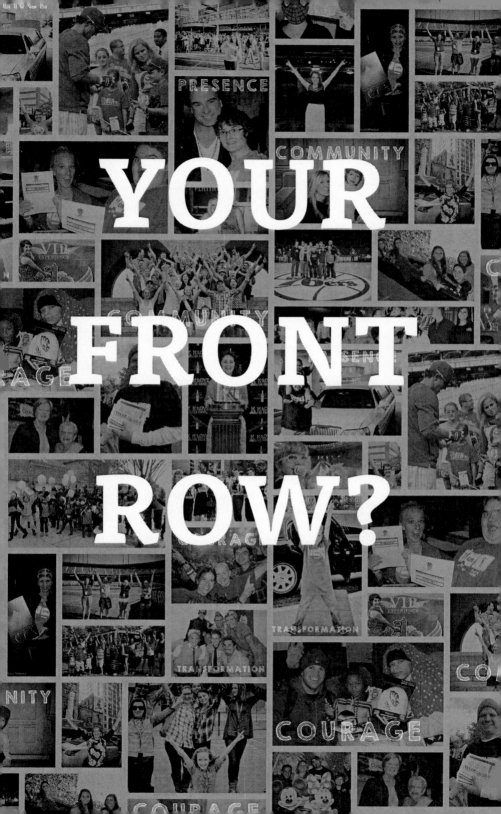

CULTIVATE EMPOWERING ENVIRONMENTS

How will you create an environment that
helps you come alive?

*My proximity to the people, places, things helping me
believe in the dream that I see within me.*

—BROTHA JAMES, Lyrics from "Front Row Anthem"

MY WIFE TATYANA AND I HAVE WORKED VERY hard to create
an empowering environment in our home. We want to live in
a space that makes us come alive.

For example, we have a door in our kitchen covered with
chalkboard paint so we can jot down messages, reminders,
quotes, questions, ideas, and dreams.

I'll never forget walking into my kitchen early one morning, eyes half open, and being surprised by a note from my wife.

Dear Jon,

Have I told you lately that I believe in you? I do. You are the most beautiful human I've ever met. You, Jon, are talented and driven. There is fire in you that is hot and good—a powerful combination. It's a real honor for me to watch you grow. You have already made so much of a difference on this planet, and you're only 40! So much to come ... Just one look at you, and I see light, greatness, wisdom, charm, focus, and motivation. I love you.

T.

Later that day, after my five-year-old son witnessed this moment, which he could clearly see I was moved by, he decided to write me a note also. It read, "You are the best pirsin in the yoonivers." Tatyana's choosing to take five minutes to write me that note made her a moment maker. She didn't even need to be present when the moment actually happened. She created a slight shift in the environment that changed the course of the entire day for the Vroman family. Perhaps it can now alter your life because I'm sharing the story. Experiences like these prompt me to ask, *How does our environment shape our experience in any given moment?*

COUNTERCLOCKWISE

Ellen Langer is a social scientist and professor of psychology at Harvard University who has explored how environments affect us. In a landmark study which took place in 1979, Langer invited a group of men in their seventies to a retreat center for a week where the environment was designed to appear as it might have around 1959, about 20 years earlier.

Every aspect of the environment was changed to support this—the magazines on the tables, past issues of newspapers, books that the men might have read. Appliances from the era included a phonograph and black-and-white TV. Langer's team encouraged the men to act in 1959-fashion: Even their conversations focused on subjects of two decades prior, and they spoke as if that year was their present. A control group of men spent the week in a place similarly designed, but they received no instructions about how to act or speak.

This extraordinary study yielded fascinating results that stunned even Langer and her research team. After just one week, the men experienced an overall improvement in well-being. Their eyesight and hearing improved, their cognitive functioning was enhanced, they felt stronger and more flexible, and their posture had improved. Even the control group, which was solely exposed to a shift in the environment, experienced similarly positive results in the same areas.

This study, along with many others by Langer, indicates that the impact lies in being aware of the ways we mindlessly react to environmental cues. Her work shows how we can actively influence any existing behaviors by making subtle changes in our daily lives. Langer says that, "It is not our physical state that limits us, it is our *mindset* about our own limits, our perceptions, that draws the lines in the sand."

We have more power over our health and well-being than we ever imagined. Knowing that your surroundings could alter your physical and mental capabilities and life experiences, how do you make the most of your environment? What are the environmental ingredients that support you and others in making the most of each and every moment?

There's an old saying, "If you hang out long enough in the barber shop, you're bound to get a haircut." Different places evoke different emotions and therefore trigger different behaviors in each of us. The people and things that surround us, change us. During my interview with Eric Davis, a former Navy SEAL sniper, we talked about the power of our environment. He said, "My environment is crafted so I can perform every day." Now, Eric is a highly disciplined guy, yet we were laughing about the fact that if someone puts beer in our fridge, we're probably going to drink it. He followed up with, "Structure determines behavior. My environment is everything and I am 100% in control of my environment."

If I take my kids to the park, it's a safe bet that they will run and play; if I take my kids to an ice cream shop, they want to eat. We create our environment and our environment creates us. If you want to improve the quality of your life and the lives of those around you, your environment cannot be ignored. Let's look at how focusing on creating a unique environment has been a critical piece for the Front Row Foundation, and the impact this focus has on our recipients and their families.

MEET FRONT ROW RECIPIENT MIKE LEIGH

Mike Leigh, also known as "Rockstar Mike," looked like a typical 19-year-old young man—tall and handsome, with a glowing smile and a terrific sense of humor. He gave great hugs and had tons of adoring fans in his hometown near Chicago. Developmentally, he was like a seven-year-old boy. Despite his long list of serious health challenges—a soft airway, an enlarged heart, pulmonary hypertension, asthma, cirrhosis of the liver, an enlarged spleen, and platelet issues—and the declining strength of his body, Mike put on a happy face.

Mike *loved* pirates. He knew every *Pirates of the Caribbean* movie word for word, and his mom said he'd wanted to be a real pirate someday. When he was a little boy, he protested a certain nightly ritual because "pirates don't brush their teeth!" When we heard about Mike's passion for pirates, our team got to work planning his Front Row experience to the best pirate show around: "Pirates Voyage" in Myrtle Beach, South Carolina.

The morning of the flight, a beautiful stretch limo picked up Mike and his family and headed for the airport. Mike had been talking about riding in this limo for weeks leading up to the event. His face lit up when he saw it in his driveway! After a quick ride to the airport, Mike was ready to board his first airplane. Excitement filled the air. Everyone, including the gate agents, was happy with and for Mike. It was wheels-up, destination Myrtle Beach!

A few hours later, the plane touched down in sunny South Carolina. The weather was picture-perfect: temperatures in the 70s, breezy, comfortable. Mike's room at the hotel had a private balcony with a view of the Atlantic Ocean that he was seeing and hearing for the first time.

When it was time for the show, a shiny black stretch SUV was waiting for everyone in front of the hotel. When Mike saw it, his jaw dropped to the ground—he could not believe his eyes. Vicki, Mike's mom, covered her mouth and began crying when she saw how excited Mike was to ride in such a cool limo. Mike felt like a real movie star pulling up to the venue. His face lit up and everyone jumped when a real pirate opened the door and yelled, "Ahoy, maties!"

Before the show started, Mike enjoyed the special pre-show event, complete with a juggling pirate, a singing pirate, and a dancing sea lion. He laughed and laughed! We caught his mom staring at him and softly smiling, taking in all his joy.

Now it was time for the big show. It was a packed house, and Mike was in the front row. Dinner was served: potato soup, buccaneer biscuits, half o' roasted cackler (chicken), mashed and flogged taters, cob o' buttery (corn), and "apple o' me eye" pie—a dinner fit for pirates.

Mike took it all in. His face glowed, and he grinned from ear to ear. It was the end of the show, but not the end of the experience for Mike. The team had arranged a special meet-and-greet where some of the pirates met with Mike and gave him a special flag with the characters' autographs. He held and stared at it for at least two minutes. He was in shock.

Mike's Front Row experience was truly magical on so many levels since he'd had so many health setbacks in the time before the event. It was a miracle that he even made the trip. Days before the trip, Mike's mom learned that he had only a short time to live. In fact, the doctors said, "He may have just a few months." In his final days of life, our board member and event coordinator Carey Smolensky told us that, upon visiting Mike at the hospital, he walked into the room and caught Mike flipping through the photo book from his Front Row experience.

Mike's story is a powerful example of how the three forces we've talked about make the moment: mindset, relationships, environment. Mike brought the right mindset—he was a raving fan of pirates. We had the right people—his family along with our event hosts to make sure every detail was handled. We had the right environment—our team making sure that every detail was thought through, from playing Mike's favorite music in the limo to having his favorite snacks. With our recipients, we even know how comfortable they are with pictures and video and adjust our approach to capture the experience while giving them privacy. Our team are experts at knowing how to spark and sustain great conversation through questions to create a fun, relaxed atmosphere.

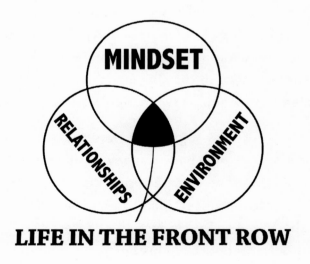

LIFE IN THE FRONT ROW

Moment makers consider every aspect of the environment to influence the experience of everyone involved. If you've thrown parties or even helped organize a wedding, you know and appreciate what I'm talking about. Mike's environment was setting everything up for success—the stretch limo, oceanfront hotel room, first plane ride, his favorite food, carefully selected gifts, and amazing seats to the show of his dreams.

By intentionally designing every detail of Mike's day, we created a new focus, and therefore new feelings and ultimately a front row moment nobody will ever forget.

LIVING LIFE IN THE FRONT ROW EVERY DAY

In 2005, the Front Row Foundation's mission was to create an incredible front row experience for the recipients; over the years we've evolved, and our purpose has expanded to serving our community by helping everyone connected with FRF live every day in the front row.

We continually look for new and imaginative ways to cultivate an environment where our recipients, their family members, donors, supporters, or anyone connected to our community can practice the art of moment making. We ask ourselves, *How can we design and create an empowering environment for each and every person to thrive?* We've answered that question by creating...

THE FRONT ROW FACTOR PODCAST:

I once heard someone say, "Turn your car into a university on wheels." Doing this became one of the most important decisions of my life. Over 20 years, I've listened to about 7,300 hours of audio programs, books, and podcasts. Learning to see my commute to work not as a waste of time but as some of the best hours of my day. This is a perfect example of reframing the perception we have of an already existing environment.

In 2016, to answer a request from our community, we started our own weekly show—The Front Row Factor Podcast. Each week I interview extraordinary people who are living life in the front row. I talk with a variety of people, including our very own recipients and family members who we've created experiences for, top donors, ambassadors—*our monthly donors*— and top supporters. We've even interviewed a magician, film maker, pro athletes, crossfit champions, UFC fighters, and so many others who are living big and giving big. We dig into the stories, science, and strategies around hope, celebration, mindset, relationships, and environment. Creating these podcasts has allowed us a way to serve our community like we never could before. You can find all episodes, notes and suggested resources at FrontRowFactor.com.

THE FRONT ROW DADS RETREAT:

For many years, I've invested time and energy attending events focused on personal and professional growth. Yet when I looked at my calendar, which should be a reflection of our values, I did not attend a single event focused on becoming the dad my kids deserved. If being a dad is my most important role, something was off. I know myself well enough to know that I would rather spend three days focused on one thing without interruption rather than taking one hour per week for an entire year. Immersion experiences build powerful momentum.

Now I host our Front Row Dads Retreat, where dads can come together twice a year to form a brotherhood, deepen their sense of purpose as fathers, and co-create optimal family strategies. It's been wildly successful. The environment we create allows for open and effective conversation. When dads take time to connect, share, and grow, they are much more likely to bring that same energy home to their kids. The challenge that most dads face is that they may spend time "in" their family, but not much time working "on" their family. Just like when we take a recipient out of their day-to-day routine and interrupt their daily patterns so that something new can emerge—we do the same for dads.

When the Front Row Dads return home after the retreat, their ability to engage, influence, and create meaningful moments with their families goes through the roof.

We work very hard to create an environment for our dads, so our dads can create the best environment for their kids. If you want to hear what the guys say about the event, check out FrontRowDads.com.

THE FRONT ROW SUMMIT

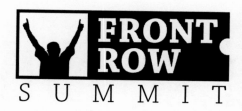

This is a unique gathering of board members, recipients, family members, donors, volunteers, staff, and others who value our mission, all coming together under one roof. For anyone wanting to take living life in the front row to the next level while helping co-create the future of the Front Row Foundation, the summit is the place to be. Our last summit, designed and facilitated by Jon Berghoff, included hikes among 300-million-year-old rocks in a National Forest, a personal visit from the co-founder of Priceline.com Jeff Hoffman, a piece of avocado toast being auctioned off for $2,500, and, when it was all said and done, four people with Front Row tattoos. Does it sound exciting? It was. Anyone can apply to attend the next summit at FrontRowFactor.com/Summit

THE BEST YEAR EVER BLUEPRINT LIVE EVENT

 +

The Front Row Foundation partnered with my buddies Hal Elrod and Jon Berghoff for an annual three-day event. The Best Year Ever Blueprint (BYEB) live event is designed to be highly experiential so that each attendee can create their personal playbook for the year and discover the fuel needed to bring their most compelling future visions to life. The event is unlike any other. Year after year, attendees never know what surprises they might encounter, but at previous events they've found anything from drum circles to professional improv training. There have been interviews with billionaires and magic shows on the same afternoon. The fun, energy, and inspiration is all mixed with actionable content, meaningful conversations, and the co-creation of your best year ever. The experience is world-class, and people return time and time again because the environment is carefully designed for each person to *come fully alive*. If you want to have your best year ever, visit FrontRowFactor.com/bye.

THE POWER OF PROXIMITY

Dr. John Norcross, an expert on behavior change and the author of *Changeology*, states, "Your environment is not defined simply by where you are; it's also characterized by the people who surround you and the situation you're in."

Where you are matters. What you see, feel, and experience matters. And *who* you're with matters. Your environment is anything in the physical realm—locations, activities, people— that affects your emotional experience, because it captures your attention and changes your experience, consciously or not. Within FRF, one of the most powerful forces at work is simply taking recipients out of their daily environment and putting them somewhere new. While allowing them to share the experience with loved ones, it also puts them in proximity with their heroes—the great moment makers of entertainment or sports who help make life special. This experience interrupts the pattern of daily life and allows space for something new to emerge. We've taken that same philosophy, which started with FRF recipients, and applied it to the Retreat, the Summit, and everything else we do.

If proximity is power, how can you shape your world, your environment, to make the most of every moment?

AUSTIN

Creating these experience for the past 11 years with Front Row Foundation has caused me to ask myself, *How can I intentionally shape my environment to create the most meaningful experiences for my family and business?*

For a few years now, my wife and I have been exploring what environment would most align with our values. We explored Richmond, Virginia; Athens, Georgia; Denver, Colorado; Temecula, California; Jupiter, Florida; Hudson, Ohio; and Portland, Oregon. At times, we'd visit areas for up to five weeks to really immerse ourselves in the culture. All were amazing cities, but in the end we wanted to make one of them home, and eventually our very last stop became our first choice. It was Austin, Texas. We've been asked a lot recently, why Austin? Three main reasons: culture, climate, and community. We felt the environment would be the best for the Vroman family to thrive. We could be happy anywhere, but we've also found it's a whole lot easier being happy in Austin. This theory has been proving true.

How do you feel about your environment now—at home, at work, within your community? Does it support your highest values? What changes would you make to bring about your highest levels of fulfillment for yourself and all those you care for?

Orison Swett Marden says, "A strong, successful man is not the victim of his environment. He creates favorable conditions." Everything in my office is designed to inspire me to do the things that are most important—right now. If something is in my line of sight, I am reminded that it's important. If anything doesn't inspire me, it's gone. It's as important and beneficial to ask what needs to be removed (to minimize distractions and direct your focus) as asking what you should add. Creating an empowering environment is about changing your outer world to align with your inner world.

In the book *The Happiness Advantage,* author Shawn Achor shared his personal struggle in fulfilling his goal of playing the guitar daily. No matter how hard he tried, the guitar remained in the case. He then tried putting the guitar in the center of his apartment, which resulted in his playing for 21 days straight. By saving the 20 seconds required to take the guitar out of the case, he made a different choice. He calls this "the 20-second rule." If something takes longer than 20 seconds to initiate, the likelihood of your doing it goes down dramatically.

Science shows we all have a limited amount of willpower, and that's why even a guy like Eric Davis, the Navy SEAL sniper I talked about earlier, has his assistant make sure his running clothes, water bottle, and keys are right by the door, so that making the right decision is that much easier. I've noticed that when my yoga mat is lying on the floor, I'll do yoga 10 times more often than if it's rolled up in the corner.

When I walk into my home office, I feel energized. I've got a standing desk and a giant wall calendar. I've decorated the walls with sticky notes with my biggest dreams and goals.

I have my Top 8 relationships written down, and next to each name is their biggest dream. By seeing this, I'm able to support them and be a raving fan in their front row. When I wake up and do my Miracle Morning routine (miraclemorning.com), I see my dreams and the dreams of those I care most about. My dreams and my friends' dreams get support, because my environment supports me first.

Each morning, I pull out a 4x6 index card and write my "High Five" activities. These are the most important tasks of the day, and I put this in plain sight. I turn off wifi and put my phone on Do Not Disturb when it's not needed, so I'm not tempted by the distraction. I set timers for 30, 60, and 90 minutes depending on the activity to remind me to take stretch breaks. I'm not sure I'm any more disciplined than anyone else, I just set myself up for success by taking ownership of my environment. Our habitat influences our habits. If freedom is what you crave, remember that structure can set you free.

A 60-DOLLAR REMINDER

On a recent trip to Amsterdam with Tatyana, we were walking down one of the gorgeous city streets lined with cool little shops. Inside one, I saw a very cool wristband. It was $60. I was sure I could buy the same wristband for $10 back home. I almost walked away, but I reminded myself that

I wasn't buying a wristband, I was buying a memory. The physical item was an emotional anchor to that moment in time.

To me, that memory was worth $60, not the wristband itself. Every time I see the wristband, it's a celebration of that experience.

It's essential that we consciously choose what we put in our front row because it influences our thinking. The rest of the world wants to advertise to us, to capture our attention. We must become the Head of Marketing for our own lives.

Think about your environment right now. Does it make you come alive? What makes you feel great? What's draining your energy? As Marie Kondo wrote in her book, *The Life Changing Magic of Tidying Up*, ask yourself about each item, "Does this spark joy?" If not, it goes.

Is your space cluttered? If you're like me, clutter can be frustrating and even depressing. It takes up physical and mental space. It can feel overwhelming and distracting. How you feel about your living space, whether you realize it or not, is having a mental impact on you. The next time you walk into a room, I invite you to ask, "How does this make me feel?" If the answer is anything but positive, make a change.

KNOW YOURSELF

Author Peter Shankman likes to say that he's been *"Diagnosed Gifted with ADHD."* During my podcast interview with him (Episode #47), I asked how he was able to publish multiple books despite ADHD. I wouldn't have guessed his answer if you'd given me 100 tries.

For his last book, he bought a plane ticket from NYC to Tokyo. He knows that he writes best on planes, so he wrote the first five chapters on the way to Japan. At the airport in Tokyo, he showered, drank two espressos, and jumped back on the plane. "I walked off the plane 31 hours later with a book in hand," he said. "You just have to know what works for you." Peter had created an environment that kept him focused.

Later during our interview, he also mentioned that, when he completes a speaking contract in Las Vegas, he commits to being in the city for no more than eight hours. Does he have a gambling or drinking problem? No. But he understands the idea that if you hang out long enough in Vegas, you're bound to roll the dice.

If you're not shaping your experience of life, someone else will happily do it for you. If you don't advertise to yourself, others will. Successful companies are hard at work creating experiences for their customers by shaping the environment. Starbucks makes sure the smell of the food doesn't over-power the smell of coffee filling the air. The music, colors, and layout are all part of the experience.

It's no accident that you find milk at the back of the grocery store. Being one of the most popular items in the store, the environment forces you to walk past other food, which increases the likelihood you'll buy more. When you do leave, the checkout lines are stacked with impulse buys like batteries, gum, and magazines.

There are smart people who know how your brain works. They know if you keep seeing something, the *law of familiarity* sets in. You get comfortable with it. You'll get curious about it. You'll likely buy or buy in. What if you could start to put the same effort into promoting to yourself?

QUESTION YOUR ENVIRONMENT

When it comes to the biggest goals, consider asking yourself, *What environment would I need to create to help me stay focused, inspired, and taking action toward getting it done in the fastest, most effective, and enjoyable way?* For example, when writing this book I didn't ask only *What time of day is best for writing?* I asked *What environment would support my writing the most?*

If you're a parent, try asking yourself, *What environment could I create for my kids that would allow them to naturally experience support in developing to their fullest potential?* For instance, just like I discussed earlier regarding the 20-second rule, by putting musical instruments in our living room, on display, my boys are far more likely to play music.

If you're looking for the partner of your dreams, try asking *Where would my ideal partner spend their time?* My bet is that, if you put yourself in that same environment, your chances of crossing paths with that type of person increases exponentially. Or you could always just get a roommate and see if that works. It did for me.

AMPLIFY THE GOOD

When I was 16, I was the proud owner of a 1982 dark green Jeep CJ7 with a tan roof and big tires. It was awesome. While I loved the Jeep, I didn't love the rattles. I remember taking little pieces of cardboard and foam to stick in corners and between metal pieces to try to stop the noise. You know what finally worked? Buying a louder stereo! I turned the volume up, and my problem was solved. I only heard music, no rattles. It was instant relief. Stress went down, happiness went up. At a young age, I was learning the value of amplifying the good to silence what's not. I was learning that if we can't change our seat, make the most of the moment. I was learning to take control of my environment. Where there's a will, there's a way.

HOW WILL YOU CREATE AN ENVIRONMENT THAT MAKES YOU COME ALIVE?

THE FRONT ROW MOVEMENT

PART FOUR

All that is important is this one moment in movement. Make the moment important, vital and worth living. Do not let it slip away unnoticed and unused..

—MARTHA GRAHAM

BUILDING MOMENTUM

How can moment making be your
new rhythm?

You are superfantastic!

—THE TOLLBOOTH LADY

SHOW ME YOUR HABITS, AND I'LL SHOW YOU your life. It's
critical to be intentional about how you invest your time.
How can you develop the habit of moment making? On one
sunny afternoon, I watched someone living the answer to this
question with courage and creativity.

THE SUPER FANTASTIC TOLLBOOTH LADY

I was cruising through Richmond, Virginia, when I pulled up to a tollbooth and was greeted by an older woman who asked me,

"Hello sweetie! How you doing today?"

I responded enthusiastically, "I'm excellent. Thank you."

She looked at me with this puzzled, even angry, look in her eyes and just paused. She then said sternly, "No!"

I felt immediately as if I had somehow said something wrong and offended her. She eventually broke the silence by smiling ear to ear and saying, "YOU. ARE. SUPERFANTASTIC!"

I started laughing. And then it was over. Just a brief encounter, yet I couldn't wipe the smile off my face.

As I drove down the road, I thought what you probably would have thought in the same situation: *Does she do this with every single driver?* I mean, if you had an eight-hour shift working at the tollbooth, how many times could you do that without losing enthusiasm? My next thought was, maybe she'd just done it for me. Maybe I was the lucky one. My ego wanted that to be true, but it's more likely that this is her thing. Then it hit me—if she did this with every single car, what an incredible impact!

I shared the superfantastic tollbooth lady story several times in the months afterward. Then one day I was watching TV and I saw a commercial. And guess who the star of the commercial was? You got it. The tollbooth lady. Her one line was, "Try it. It's Superfantastic!!!" I'll never forget that moment. I stood up in my living room and started screaming at the TV, "You did it. You're famous!" While simply being famous isn't always a great indicator of value, in that moment, I was celebrating her impact.

Watching her on TV taught me that you can approach life in one of two ways. You can choose to be a victim or a victor. She could have said, "I work a tollbooth—*I can't really make a difference.*" She would then choose to be the victim. Instead she saw her work as an opportunity to make a *huge* difference—she chose to be the victor. You either see oppression or opportunity. The world is filled with both. I'm not saying you're never the victim or experiencing oppression, but the one thing others can't control is your focus and response.

The proof is not that she simply starred in a commercial, but that, fifteen years later, I'm telling you this story. She had ten seconds with me at a tollbooth, but I've told her story 10,000 times. This tollbooth lady chose to use each moment to make the biggest impact in the way she could—*every day*. By doing so, she created a front row moment for me that would shape my future forever. It's fun to think about how many lives she touched. One by one, day by day. Her daily rhythm was being a moment maker for others using her current resources. Never underestimate the ability that you have to make a lasting, meaningful impact on someone's life, even with just three words.

YOU. ARE. SUPERFANTASTIC!

MEET FRONT ROW RECIPIENT
KELSEY BISHOP

Full of zest and compassion, Kelsey Bishop is a superfantastic young lady who has accomplished a lot in her life. She's the definition of genuine, and her brightness and glow make it all too easy to fall in love with her.

When she was 22 years old, she was diagnosed with acute myeloid leukemia (AML). AML is a type of cancer that starts inside the bone marrow, the soft tissue inside bones that helps form blood cells. The cancer grows from cells that would normally turn into white blood cells, and it progresses quickly without proper treatment.

It was during her treatment that Kelsey began falling in love with the star of her chosen event (I can't reveal the event because of confidentiality agreements). Inspiration, laughter, smiles, and hope filled Kelsey whenever she'd watch a show.

A nursing student and full-time worker at the ER, Kelsey was forced to resign her positions and enter full time in-patient treatment. Her friends and family were always inspired by her day-to-day positivity. She said this during a post-event interview:

I love experiences. I will take an experience over a gift any day. That was what I was thinking the whole time I was there.

This is an amazing gift—I will have these memories for a lifetime. A bag, or a gift card, or money, it just passes away. This is a true gift. An experience.

That is one thing I have carried with me since having my front row experience is I try to create experiences for other people as gifts because it's a lasting memory and it's a gift that keeps giving.

Kelsey is a moment maker. She understands the value of experiences over things. In fact, researchers interviewed more than 150 people about recent purchases and found that spending money on activities such as concerts or being with friends at restaurants brought much more pleasure than material purchases.[16]

I love that Kelsey takes ownership of her daily life by creating experiences for others. She's created a *habit* of being a moment maker. She's *chosen* to make contribution part of her *rhythm of life*.

I remember, years ago, being deeply moved by the words of author Victor Frankl, who wrote in *Man's Search for Meaning* about one's *daily* approach to life.

Everything can be taken from a man but one thing: the last of the human freedoms—to choose one's attitude in any given set of circumstances, to choose one's own way. When we are no longer able to change a situation, we are challenged to change ourselves. Between stimulus and response there is a space. In that space is our power to choose our response. In our response lies our growth and our freedom.

Kelsey, the tollbooth lady, Frankl and so many others you've read about in this book have *chosen the habit* of making the most of each moment and creating the best possible outcome based on their resources. They've consciously established positive rituals, rhythms, and routines for both living and giving.

MAXIMIZING MOMENTS

Since tomorrow is guaranteed to nobody, I want to make today count and take nothing for granted. As a result, I'm obsessed with time management and productivity. As a rather silly example, I once calculated how long it took me to walk from our kitchen table to get the saltshaker. It was 22 seconds. Let's do some quick math here. If it's 22 seconds x 4 days per week I get the salt, and this happens every week for the next 40 years, that's a total of 50 hours of my life walking to get salt. Do you know what I could get done in 50 hours? What if I just bought a second salt shaker and kept it on the table?

Because I don't *love* walking to get the salt, then the second shaker frees up time for me to do things that I do love. What difference would it make if I invested that 50 hours reading books with my son? What if I spent that 50 hours writing love notes to people I care about? What if I were to meditate for 50 hours?

What are 10 other areas of my life where I could save that time? That would be 500 hours of extra time.

MOMENTUM

Adam Braun, founder of *Pencils of Promise* said, "For any movement to gain momentum, it must start with small action," and Aesop famously said "No act of kindness, no matter how small, is ever wasted."

Moment by moment, we build momentum.

In my podcast interview with Jim Sheils, the author of *The Family Board Meeting*, we got into a conversation about daily habits—which he calls *rhythms*. Specifically, we were talking about how he schedules a "board meeting" with each of his children every 90 days. These meetings are free from electronics, last for a minimum of four hours, and are focused on quality time together. The minute one is done, they're already looking forward to the next one. It's a brilliant rhythm that ensures that front row moments are happening with his kids.

For a time, I rejected rhythms in my life because they felt like the antithesis of the freedom and variety I craved, but then I heard someone say, "Systems set you free." Systems are just another word to describe our habits, routines, or rhythms. I'm constantly asking, *Which rhythms will help myself and others make the most of every moment?*

MORNING RHYTHMS

One of my most important rhythms is my Miracle Morning routine. It's a simple practice with six actions—Silence, Affirmations, Visualization, Exercise, Reading, and Scribing (Journaling)—otherwise know as the Life S.A.V.E.R.S.

**Before I make moments for others,
I take a moment for myself.**

The man behind the Miracle Morning, my buddy Hal, has told me, "When you win the morning, you win the day." During my journaling time, I ask morning questions (I shared these in chapter 8). The most important question is, *How will I be a moment maker today?*

DAILY RHYTHMS

While each day is very different, there *are* rhythms. I live by some very simple guidelines. Here are a few examples. I'm committed to sweating daily. I love to run, so many days I'm on the trails near my home. Some days I'll do yoga or swim. Occasionally, I'll just hit the sauna. No matter what, I sweat.

Next, I work best in blocks of time. I'll typically focus for 45–90 minutes, depending on the project. I'm constantly taking breaks and shifting my environment, so I'm either stimulating creativity or focusing my attention. I put a great deal of attention on having healthy foods and clean water to fuel my front row life. I meditate regularly, even if only for 30 seconds. Most often, it's 5–7 minutes repeated two or three times throughout the day.

Last, I ask myself questions regularly and mindfully, one of the most important being, *How can I recognize or create a front row moment right now?*

EVENING RHYTHMS

The evenings are a time of reflection and celebration. After we've wrapped up the day, it's time to wind down. Living a front row life isn't always about being level 10 at a rock concert. There is great joy at looking back on the day and asking, *What were my front row moments today?*

I grab my front row journal and document the best moments. I ask my family about their moments. I've also shared with my kids that front row moments can be challenging moments where we learned something. **Often, our failures are our front row moments in disguise.** They teach us something important. Failure often comes after we step up with courage and try something new. The act of exploration and discovery is to be celebrated.

Living fully requires a fully charged battery. "Taking a stand" during the day means lying down at night. I'd love to think, "I'll sleep when I'm dead." As much as I don't want to sleep my life away, and as much as I think "Live every day like it's my last," the truth is—and statistics back me up—that tomorrow is likely coming, and it's going to be a whole lot better if I'm rested. Life is a marathon, not a sprint, so taking care of you is a huge part of the front row factor. I used to think sleep got in the way of making moments, but now I realize that sleep is what fuels them.

"Our lives change when our habits change" says my friend Matthew Kelly. What daily habits and rhythms would most support you living life in the front row? What rhythms can you put in place today that support you being a moment maker? What are the most powerful questions you must constantly ask yourself to stay focused on what matters most?

What rhythms help you make the most of every moment?

BE A MOMENT MAKER

The Front Row Family—*It's a Forever Thing*

THE ENCORE

Happiness [is] only real when shared

—JON KRAKAUER, *Into the Wild*

ONE HOT SUMMER NIGHT IN SHELL LAKE, WISCONSIN, our family gathered around in the living room, as we did each night while at the lake house, telling stories and eating homemade Oreo cookie ice cream. Out of nowhere, I heard a loud booming voice from outside. "Jonathan Vroman!"

I heard it again, this time a bit louder: "JONATHAN VROOOOOOOOOMAN." As I ran to the front door, I saw two adults with sheets over their heads carrying torches. Underneath the makeshift costumes stood my dad and his brother—my Uncle John. I walked to meet them and, under their orders, marched side by side with them down the gravel driveway until we entered a musty cabin filled with daddy longlegs, giant moths colliding with the windows in an attempt to escape, and a concrete floor with just a couple of old throw rugs.

In the 1940s and 50s, it was used as an icehouse, but since then it had become home for two sets of bunk beds, a few homemade swords, a broken slingshot, and even a model pirate ship. This building was where the boys slept while at the camp. The girls had their own cabin as well—theirs was the GLH. None of the boys knew what that meant, but suspected it was "Girls Laughing House." The boys cabin is called the FHA, and, up until that day, I had no idea what that stood for; to know, you had to be a member . . . and guess what was about to happen next?

While I can't reveal every detail about my induction or what the FHA means—I've been sworn to secrecy—I can tell you vividly how I felt in that moment when I became a member. My father and I sat down at a small wooden table, looking across at each other as he shared the history and traditions of the FHA, and how he became a member himself when he was 13. As he spoke, I hung on his every word. I was accepted as an official FHA member that day. It was a coming-of-age moment. I felt loved. I felt worthy. I learned what those three simple letters stood for, why they're so important, and what it means to be not only a Vroman, but part of this club.

Perhaps that moment grew into the deep desire I have to make people feel welcomed, loved, and part of the "club." It's events like this that provided not only a map, but the fuel needed to be a moment maker for others today. Experiences are often anchors to values and beliefs that guide our lives. In hindsight, I can clearly see the brilliance of how this moment shaped my mindset. At the time, I was just a 10-year-old boy with his dad, totally in the moment. While the actual moment may not have lasted long, the memory has never escaped.

> It was a moment in time, but it was the time of my life.

IT'S A FAMILY THING

I love you.

I can say that confidently and truthfully because I see the world in two groups:

1. There are people I know and love.

2. There are people I love, but have yet to know.

I'm not saying I like everyone the same, but as a member of team human, I love people in general because my belief system says that underneath whatever they do or say is a soul that wants the same things as you and I. People want love, connection, and significance.

I also know at a fundamental level that if you thrive in healthy ways, my kids have a better chance for the same. You, my friend, are shaping the world my children are growing up in. Every word you speak and action you take either helps or hurts humanity. I want you to succeed, not just for you or me, but my fatherly instincts kick in and I want that so much for my kids. We're connected deeply and, by lifting each other up, everyone is elevated.

We want everyone in the Front Row community to feel like family, and that's why we emphasize —*the Front Row family*.

With every recipient experience, we want the families we serve to feel loved, from the minute they learn about the Front Row Foundation until the end of time. That's why one of our event coordinators, Kaile Monroe, says—*it's a forever thing*.

Theresa Casey shared the impact one of our team members continues to have on her family, even after the event for her late husband, Chris Casey:

I remember when I first met Shannon, she had said, "You're part of the family now." She was always coming by our home.

She came by one time and was dropping off homemade salad dressing. Then she gave us a beautiful framed picture of the six of us from that day. There was always something. She showed up the day before Chris passed. She showed up at the hospital. She just walked in. She's like, "Hey." She brought pastries. "Just wanted to see everybody and give everybody a hug." Chris's sisters were blown away. They just couldn't believe that she was there. I said, "You know what? I'm not because she has not stopped caring from the moment I met her." I was not surprised at any of that because she was always in touch with us or sending a positive message. "I'm thinking of you, I'm praying for you." All along. It was wonderful. I didn't know what she meant when she first said, "You're part of our family."

———————

I love that the front row experiences we create often begin with one simple moment in time, yet become so much more over the years. Shannon continues to be a moment maker for the Casey family. She chooses to stand by, with, and for them.

SHOW UP EVERY DAY

My parents are incredible people. I feel their love and support daily. They have shown up my entire life. I'm grateful for this. I don't take it for granted. They've been moment makers for me more times than I can count.

Around age 19, I was going through a tough time in life. My parents knew it. One day while I was visiting my dad, he asked, "Have you seen the movie *Rudy*?" I hadn't. He continued, "You've gotta watch it." I told him I couldn't afford to. In fact, I had just sold one of my favorite childhood baseball cards to put gas in the tank. In that moment, my dad handed me $5.00 and made me promise that I'd rent it. I did. And if you haven't seen the movie, it's epic.

My dad showed up with a timely gift of $5.00 and a movie suggestion—and in that moment the course of my life was altered. Did he know in that moment it would have such an impact? No. Did *I* know in that moment it would have such an impact? No. How many opportunities will you have to be a moment maker for someone important in your life today? Each opportunity has the potential to be *the* moment that changes everything. The key is to keep showing up for people and making moments count—every. single. day.

While we're talking movies and showing up for people, in the film *Mad Max: Fury Road*, there is a scene that illustrates these concepts powerfully. In this scene, there was a man who was going to sacrifice his life to take out some bad guys. Just before he leapt to his death, he looked at his fellow warriors and yelled, "Witness me!" His fellow fighters looked back and screamed, "Witness him!" They all watched as he courageously gives his life for his brothers. After he is gone, they all yell, "Witnessed!"

That scene gives me chills. I think it portrays our deep human desire to be witnessed—to be valued—to feel worthy of another's attention, recognition, and love.

In the Front Row Foundation, we believe deeply that every person's life is worth witnessing and celebrating. I think I learned this from my parents early on, everytime they *showed up*. They witnessed my life.

The simple act of giving your attention—of witnessing, or acknowledging, of loving—is priceless.

We can all be moment makers for others by being a witness to their lives. Today, and every day, let someone know...

I see you.

I value you.

I honor you.

I appreciate you.

I celebrate you.

There are many ways to do this. That is the *art* of being a moment maker.

STAND FOR OTHERS

Living a front row life is about choosing who and what you'll stand for. Stepping up for people, especially in tough situations, takes courage. Sometimes it's hard to know who's being impacted more when you take a stand. And I use the word stand as a metaphor. I'm talking about emotionally rising to the occasion, fully engaging and bringing your best to each and every moment, for each and every person.

There is a super talented dance group that performs in Vegas called the Jabbawockeez. Years ago, I saw them perform live; at the end of the show, everyone was clapping and yelling, but I noticed that there was no standing ovation. What was wrong with this crowd? As soon as I started judging everyone else, I had to turn the question on myself—*Why am I not standing?* I knew exactly why. It was fear. What if I stand and I'm the only one?

I decided to stand, and there I was, the only one in a crowd of 1,000, giving a standing ovation. Typically, when one person stands, others join in. Not this time. It was just me. So, do I just sit back down? I decided to just stand there. I was standing for the performers because they earned it. I was also taking a stand for that quiet inner voice that says,

Follow your heart. Do what is right, not what is popular.

Just when I thought it was all over, one other person stood, then everyone stood. I remember my first reaction was *Look at what I did!* Then I noticed my ego taking hold and turned my attention back to the stage when one of the lead dancers put his hands together in a prayer position and bowed in my direction as if to say, "Thank you, we worked hard for that."

Moment makers show up when the moment matters most.

When you take a stand in life, you're often the spark for others to do the same.

It's been said, "How we do one thing is how we do anything." For me, this standing ovation experience was one moment in time representing every moment in time.

How could I more proactively take a stand for others?

THE FIRST TIME

When is the last time you did something for the first time? Firsts are almost always front row moments. These moments hold special power because you can only experience *firsts* one time. They are to be anticipated and savored. One of the easiest ways to be a moment maker is to be on the lookout for opportunities to experience yourself or create experiences for others where firsts are involved. During a podcast interview with children's author Jenna Bayne, she talked about how we learn; one of those ways is through novelty or, as I'm sharing, *firsts*.

Having children has given me many opportunities to experience our boys' first smiles, steps, and words. Once I was biking with my son Tiger at Fairmount Park in Philadelphia. On this day we biked the longest we had ever gone, about five miles. Exhausted, we stopped along a stream that ran next to the bike trail. Covering the ground were thousands of rocks. I started showing Tiger how to "skip stones" on the water. He tried and tried with no luck.

Discouragement was setting in, but he kept after it. About 30 minutes later, he skipped his first stone. He was fired up. As we were walking back to the bikes, he turned around and he said to me, "Papa, I'm really proud of myself." Those are some of the best words that I have ever heard. For many of us, firsts represent a moment of progress, change and accomplishment.

> **Who would you need to be in order to have more firsts in your life?**
>
> **How can you help others create firsts today?**
>
> **Moment makers understand the power of firsts.**

Robin Littman said this about her daughter's experience at the live viewing of *The Big Bang Theory* TV show and a very powerful first:

Later on in the taping, the gentleman who was emceeing this said, "You know, we've noticed something very special about the Big Bang audiences in that they have a real fervor about this show, and that there's something that they personally connect with. Would anybody like to talk about that?" The next thing I know I hear him saying, "Yes young lady, would you like to come up here?" I look over and it's Rachel who has her hand raised, bolts past me, runs up the aisle, across the other, down the side, comes to the front, grabs the microphone, and starts talking about what *The Big Bang Theory* means to her.

This is a child who is incredibly shy around strangers, has never stood up in front of anybody and said anything, and has never been in a situation where she had to perform solo, like in music or sports or whatnot. We could not believe it. If I recall correctly, her words were something to the effect of, "People with special needs tend to feel out of step with the rest of the world. We feel different. This show is all about being different, and how acceptable it is, and that's why I like to watch it." People all applauded her. She came and sat back down, and I think John and I stared at her more the rest of the show than we stared at the show. We had never seen that courage in her before, and that ability to say, "This is who I am," to people outside of our family.

It started something in her that has not stopped. It was a truly life changing event for her.

––––––––––

What will you try that you've never done before? I love the question, *What would you attempt if you knew you could not fail?*

Observing the courage of our recipients has challenged the way I live. Seeing how each of our recipients fully embrace front row moments challenges me to do the same.

MESSY MOMENTS

Being a moment maker can feel like a lot of pressure. I'm sure there are days when the tollbooth lady doesn't feel like shouting "Superfantastic!" I often wonder if, over time, she felt a certain pressure to perform each day. What stress is involved with being a moment maker day in and day out? I've come to learn that at times being a moment maker is both meaningful and messy.

Each year, when New Year's comes around, I panic. Why? I know the holiday is important to my wife. I stress about how to make the day special. It's like the game-winning shot: Someone throws me the ball, and under pressure I choke. It feels like there's so much on the line that it's hard to make it great.

With my children and holidays like Christmas or birthdays, I'm concerned that I'm giving too many gifts and I'll spoil them, or perhaps I'm not giving enough gifts, creating enough special moments, and they won't feel appreciated. Should there be a budget? Should I give more experiences and fewer material items? Should I give money and let them pick out a gift themselves so they get exactly what they want, or should I just pick out something and lean on "It's the thought that counts"?

When it comes to gatherings like a wedding or simply a house party, there are so many things to think about—budget, attire, menu, location, invitations, and the list goes on. It's not hard to see where being a moment maker can have its challenges.

At Front Row Foundation, each event takes more than 250 hours to complete, and can come with numerous challenges. Our checklist for each experience contains more than 300 tasks that need to be done. To create an experience like our team does involves transportation, meals, concerts, games, gifts, photos, videos, and other surprises. Things don't always go according to plan, and for our staff, there's a tremendous amount of pressure to make things perfect. During the event, a million questions race through their minds—is the camera battery charged, is the microphone turned on, does the recipient need anything, and what else could be done to make this special?

There's no doubt moment making has the potential to be messy. It's important to remember that your job is to find the meaning in the mess, which can really test your skills in the art of moment making.

How can you further train your mind and heart to see every situation, positive or not, as a gift, a resource, a lesson, or a clue toward a better life? How can you condition yourself to see even more of the brilliance in every moment—especially in the challenging ones? How can you build the rhythm in your life to further recognize or create more front row moments?

I've heard it said, "Life isn't happening to you, it's happening for you." I invite you to see that everything that happens to you comes with a gift, and it's your job to figure out what it is. Moment making can be messy and meaningful at the same time.

What front row moment can you recognize or create right now?

THE FRONT ROW MOMENT EXPERIMENT

How can you be a daily moment maker and inspire others?

See now the power of truth; the same experiment which at first glance seemed to show one thing, when more carefully examined, assures us of the contrary.

— GALILEO GALILEI

NINA PEREZ IS A PROUD MOTHER AND THE owner of Baila Vancouver Dance School; she lives in Vancouver, Canada. After attending our annual Front Row Summit, Nina decided that she wanted more front row moments in her life and that she needed to make it part of her daily routine. She challenged herself to document one front row moment every day for the next 180 days. She made this commitment publicly and began her experiment immediately. Over the coming weeks, she'd post pictures to her Facebook page of her front row moments, most often with her three-year-old son Gavin. Here are a few I remember seeing:

> Her nephew taking his first steps
> Cooking with her "favorite sous chef" Gavin
> Finding snow that had melted into the shape of a heart
> Having a dance party in the car
> Receiving a text message "You are loved"

I was blown away by Nina's experiment. She inspired me to notice and create more front row moments in my own life. Deeply curious about Nina's experience, I asked her a few questions and received these brilliant answers.

Q: Why did you commit to 180 days?

A: To make it part of our life philosophy it had to be over 100 days so that it could really become a habit. I feel that anything smaller will only give you a taste, but for it to be part of your life, it needs to be long enough to become permanent.

Q: How do you define a front row moment?

A: Initially we had these criteria:

1. A moment we were feeling good

2. A moment Gavin and I would be engaged with each other

3. A moment of courage, presence, or fun

As we continued with the experiment, I realized that having self-awareness and appreciation could turn little tiny moments into epic front row moments, and this helped us through many times when the challenge became difficult. So now *any* moment that we *appreciate* is a front row moment. Appreciation defined as *the recognition and enjoyment of the good qualities of something or someone.*

Q: How did you approach each day?

A: Gavin and I would ask each morning, *what would make today great?* We'd plan out what would make certain parts of the day front row moments. That gave us a mindset to amplify the good throughout the day. We would continually ask: Is *this* a front row moment? What is good about *this* moment? What do we *love* about this moment?

I also noticed that capturing front row moments early in the day removed any stress of having to do it later. It allowed us then to experience more front row moments that we would just keep to ourselves. Sharing our experiment was the first order of focus.

Each day, we would slow down and allow all our senses to experience each moment. This would turn mundane moments into front row moments.

> **When we gave ourselves the opportunity to *savor* our reality, front row moments were in abundance.**

Q: What have you learned along the way?

A: There really are no rules, just guidelines. The whole point is to get the essence of the activity.

Over time, my life philosophy started changing and my mindset and behavior, along with Gavin's, became consistently more positive. I wasn't overwhelmed anymore. We were living more in alignment with our values.

Our front row moment experiment is now shaping our life trajectory. New opportunities, people and possibilities are all coming our way because of our new front row lifestyle.

Q: What has been the biggest benefit from this experiment?

A: It's self-awareness. I'm learning so much about myself, about Gavin, and our time together. My previous feelings of depression and overwhelm are gone. If I do have any of those feelings they only last hours instead of weeks. Gavin has had fewer tantrums or meltdowns, and everyone notices how happy he is.

Q: Was there anything positive that came from this that totally surprised you?

A: I'm surprised by how many people were paying attention to our daily posts and how it's inspiring them. My mom was even happier seeing our daily pictures and videos. I noticed that our front row moments added happiness to their lives.

People tell me "I've heard about you and Gavin!" It's fun hearing the lingo used in my community; for example, one of my dance students said to me, "What a *front row moment* that was when I pulled off that double spin in front of the whole class."

Friends who saw Gavin and me as examples decided to start their own front row moment experiment.

Q: Any advice to those who may take on this experiment?

A: Life can be paradoxical, so I'll give you two. First, *lower the bar*. A front row moment can be simple. It can be small. Living all by itself is magnificent.

Next is to *raise the bar*. Noticing life's moments on a daily basis will take some effort. Challenge yourself. I promise it will yield unimaginable rewards—love, connection, relationships, and self-awareness.

———

Throughout Nina's experiment, she's learned and shared some incredibly powerful concepts that I want to bring attention to.

Asking Quality Questions: Each morning she'd ask *What front row moments can we create today?* This primed her mind to be on the lookout. During the day she'd ask, *Is this a front row moment,* or *What's great about this moment?* The best answers always follow the best questions.

Being Held Accountable: She made a commitment to people she didn't want to let down. This helped hold her accountable. She had leverage to succeed. Her accountability buddy was her son Gavin. The more accountability you stack on, the better chance you have at winning.

Raise and Lower the Bar: When Nina would fail, she'd learn the lesson and move on. She learned to capture the essence of the activity and practiced forgiveness with herself when things didn't go according to plan. If you miss a day, you just keep going. She also had to raise the bar at times. When you are slacking off, or giving in too easily, you need to hold yourself to a higher standard. The art of moment making is about experimenting between easing up and lowering the bar to create a win and raising the bar to set a new standard.

Setting a Big Goal: By choosing 180 days, Nina gave herself a chance to form a new permanent rhythm. She and Gavin conditioned their minds and hearts to forever notice and create front row moments. Over the course of their lives, and those they impact, how much more fulfillment will they experience?

LET'S EXPERIMENT

What would life look like for you if you could recognize and create daily front row moments for yourself and others? How much more purpose and meaning could you bring to each and every moment?

**You are invited to be a daily moment maker
for the next 8 days.**

Starting today, document and share one front row moment each day for the next 8 days. We've heard countless stories from people in our community who've experienced deeply positive and profound benefits after just 8 days of capturing front row moments. Will you commit to being a moment maker for the next 8 days?

Here are a few comments from those who've taken on the 8-day experiment:

> *This is the first social media challenge that has changed the way I see my day and show up in it, and in just 8 days. I'm noticing more meaningful moments, finding meaning where I wasn't before, and I now enter my days with anticipation and focus to create them more intentionally. I am changed, and feel great energy to continue on to see how much more I can get out of this if I make it a routine*
>
> —Andrew Smallwood

The level to which this community has embraced the experiment definitely exceeded my expectations and has dominated my conversations with friends and family. Whenever I'm with them they are constantly asking me if I captured my #frontrowmoment yet. I love that! It's so contagious.

—Ramon Rouse

This daily routine of finding and acknowledging front row moments created accountability for my well being. It isn't always easy to see the positive, and being determined to create it requires activity rather than passivity. But in doing so it forced me to pull myself out of a routine of often nonproductive or negative thinking. Acknowledging at least one moment made me realize that there were far more moments I was taking for granted. I shall continue because to establish a routine takes more than eight days

—Robin Littman

MAKING HABITS STICK

On average, it takes approximately 66 days to form a new habit.

The true length depends greatly on the person, what habit's being formed, and additional circumstances. It may only take one week—it could also take one year.

An experiment published in the *European Journal of Social Psychology* conducted by Phillippa Lally that followed 96 people over 12 weeks found on average it takes about 2 months to form a new habit.[7]

Another important note: The researcher team found that even if you mess up every now and then, it's not going to change the time needed to change the habit. It's not about perfection, it's about progress.

After taking on the 8-day Front Row Moment Experiment, many in our community have committed to 8 weeks. While 8 days will be great place to start, if you really want to ensure you've created a new daily rhythm, you may find that 8 weeks is a sweet spot. It's short enough that anyone can participate, and it's long enough to help build a true rhythm into your life. Personally, I've found that in order for a new rhythm to stick in my life, I need somewhere between 45–90 days. 8 weeks gives you 56 days, and for many this is a perfect length of time.

Some of you may be thinking about committing even longer. Nina chose 180 days—why? She really wanted to create a new rhythm in her life what would stick.

Whether it's 8 days, 8 weeks, or 180 days, I invite you to join others in our community and be part of the Front Row Moment Experiment in hopes that you realize the benefits that so many others have and ultimately become a partner in the Front Row Moment *Movement*.

Our goal in this experiment transcends the nature of the temporary commitment inherent in it. Meaning, what starts as an experiment for you builds your confidence and enthusiasm to join what is already a life philosophy for others just like yourself. A way to maximize your life experience well beyond the experiment itself.

Whether you call this experiment a challenge, goal, or commitment, the essence is that you're elevating your life and the lives of those around you by experimenting with something new. Reading this now, you may already be a moment maker—awesome!—but now your job is to tweak your daily practice and refine it. There is always another level of mastery. If you're brand new, perfect! *This* is a moment when you get to choose a new adventure. Are you ready to get started?

Step 1: Get the Front Row Moment Experiment Quick Start Kit

Visit FrontRowFactor.com/experiment and download your free *Front Row Moment Experiment Quick Start Kit*. This will give you a daily tracker and journal along with other supplies that will support your experiment. Take a moment now and go download this quickly. Whether you decided to take on 8 days or 8 weeks, this is where you'll begin.

Step 2: Today, document one front row moment.

Starting now, document your first #FrontRowMoment. Want to see some examples to get you started? Our community is most active on Facebook, and by using this hashtag you can search hundreds of other front row moments to both like and comment to encourage others or simply to gain inspiration. When you download your Quick Start Kit, you'll get a personal invite to our community page.

Step 3: Put a reminder somewhere you'll see it so you remember to do this each day.

It could be an alarm on your phone, written into your calendar, or scribbled with lipstick or dry erase marker on your bathroom mirror. Creating a new habit or rhythm takes time, so give yourself every possible advantage.

Step 4: Find an accountability partner.

Hundreds of experiments later, I've noticed that when someone has an accountability partner, they're far more likely to follow through. It's not only more fun to share this experience, it's more effective. Who do you know that would value this experiment? Invite them to join you right now. Take bold action in this very moment.

To help ensure you recognize or create one front row moment each day, here's the secret sauce.

THE MOMENT MAKER'S THREE ESSENTIAL QUESTIONS EACH DAY

1. **In the morning:** What front row moments do I want to experience today?

2. **During the day:** What front row moments can I recognize or create right now?

3. **At night:** What front row moments can I celebrate today?

Let's dig a little deeper.

Each Morning:

Moment makers think ahead. Set your intentions to both recognize and create great moments. Ask future-focused questions, which set the stage for great moments to occur.

Play with the questions and see what feels good to you. Remember it's the essence of the experiment that matters most—you being a moment maker. Design questions that make you come alive! Consider asking, *What would make today great? What would an ideal day look like? Who can I serve today? How will I make the most of each and every moment?*

Every Day:

Moment makers are constantly looking to recognize and create the brilliance and opportunity in each and every moment. Continually ask powerful questions, which changes the lens by which you see the world. Fully embrace the power of the present moment.

Consider asking, *What is great about this moment? How could I make this moment even better? How can I elevate this moment for the benefit of everyone involved?*

Evening:

Moment makers recognize their wins and learn from their failures. By bringing attention to the gift in each moment, you learn and grow. Value looking back and reliving great moments to further anchor them into your memory. Bring the power of the past into the present moment.

Consider asking, *what was great about today? What can we celebrate? What were the highlights? What were the gifts in the challenges?*

> The art of moment making is asking for *what you want* and making the most of *what you get*.

ARE YOU READY?

Join us for the Front Row Moment Experiment now. If you didn't already, go to FrontRowFactor.com/experiment and download your quick start kit.

As you begin your experiment, if this book was valuable to you, who else do you know that would benefit from reading it? Share your copy with them. You could not only be a moment maker in that instant, but by giving them what's inside the book, you'd share the gift that helps them make moments forever.

What would a world full of moment makers look like? What would society look and feel like if seven billion people woke up each day asking, *How could I be a moment maker today?* and throughout their day walked around asking *How could I recognize or create a front row moment right now?* and at the end of each day asking, *What front row moments can be celebrated?* For me, I see a world where people are fully present, acting with love, and elevating humanity.

YOUR FUTURE

There are a few things I can do really well, but predicting the future isn't one of them. When I look back on my life, most of the significant moments I never saw coming. The things I wanted to happen never did, and things I didn't want to happen did. Gifts became challenges and challenges became gifts. Strangers became friends and friends became strangers. My environment changed me and I changed my environment. So my track record for predicting the future is terrible, which is why today my focus is on being a moment maker now. That is the only thing 100 percent in my control.

Living life in the front row is a metaphor for getting close to what inspires you. The front row philosophy is about connecting deeply with the people, places, and things that make you come alive. It's about finding YOUR front row in life. Just remember that being a moment maker is about being a meaning maker.

You make the moment.

You give it meaning.

You define your life.

You create your story.

Now—this moment is yours—
how will you make the most of it?

Your friend and fan,

Jon

YOU ARE

A MOMENT

MAKER.

P.S. SPECIAL NOTE TO YOU, THE MOMENT MAKER

NEVER FORGET THAT YOU ARE WORTHY OF A front row life. One of the biggest reasons why people won't live a front row life is that their current belief system tells them they're not worthy of one, and so the moment slips by unnoticed. They believe that by giving up their moment, others can have theirs. They may even forgo creating a moment for others because they don't feel they're going to do a good enough job. I get it. I still struggle with this personally at times. If I have a front row seat, someone else doesn't. If I play big, someone else might feel small. If I stand up, someone might not be able to see. If I give a gift, someone might not like it.

Sometimes our greatest gift to others is in showing them how to enjoy the front row and inviting them along. When we demonstrate self-worth, others can model it. Marianne Williamson famously said, "Your playing small does not serve the world. There is nothing enlightened about shrinking so that other people won't feel insecure around you. We are all meant to shine, as children do." You teach others how to treat themselves by how you treat yourself.

So when I ask you to step up into your front row, I'm not condoning greed; I'm voting for value. Your value. No, you don't *deserve* a front row seat, but you are worthy of the pursuit of one. If you've ever battled with self-worth, as I have, consider this.

Is a baby worthy of love? Can people love a baby completely without the baby ever doing a single thing beyond existing? Is there anything a baby can do to make itself more valuable as a human being other than being itself?

> **Just like a baby, there is nothing you'll ever do in your life that will make you more valuable *as a human being* than you are right now. You may increase the value you add to the world by what you create and share, but your value as a human will never change.**

You are enough, my friend. Never forget that. You are worthy of the pursuit of a front row life. And, just to be clear, being enough doesn't mean we stop learning, growing, and progressing. Enough means your *value as a human* is a level 10 already—and nothing you do can change that.

ENDNOTES

1   Rajendra S. Sisodia, David B. Wolfe, and Jagdish N. Sheth, *Firms of Endearment: How World-Class Companies Profit from Passion and Purpose*, Upper Saddle River, N.J.: Wharton School Publishing, 2007, p. 14.

2   Michael E. Porter and Mark R. Kramer, "The Big Idea: Creating Shared Value," Huffington Post, January 28, 2011 (reprinted from Harvard Business Review, January–February 2011).

3   Shane Lopez, *Making Hope Happen: Create the Future You Want for Yourself and Others*, New York: Simon and Schuster, 2013, p. 144.

4   Bridge, D.J., & Voss, J.L. (2014). Hippocampal binding. Journal of Neuroscience, 34(6): 2203-2213 (http://www.jneurosci.org./content/jneuro/34/6/2203.full.pdf)

5   Martin E. P. Seligman, T. A. Steen, N. Park, et al., "Positive Psychology Progress: Empirical Validation of Interventions," American Psychologist, 60 (2005), pp. 410–421.

6   Gretchen Rubin, "A New, Quick, Easy Way to Keep a Non-Journal," Psychology Today, August 7, 2009.

7   Barbara Fredrickson, Positivity: Groundbreaking Research Reveals How to Embrace the Hidden Strength of Positive Emotions, Overcome Negativity, and Thrive. New York: Crown, 2009.

8   Kenneth E. Vail, J. Uhl, J. Arndt, et al., "When Death Is Good for Life: Considering the Positive Trajectories of Terror Management," Personality and Social Psychology Review 16(4), April 2012, pp. 303–29.

9   Alia J. Crum and Ellen J. Langer, "Mind-Set Matters: Exercise and the Placebo Effect," Psychological Science 18, no. 2, 2007, pp. 165–171.

10   The study was published in Abiola Keller, Kristin Litzelman, Lauren E. Wisk, et al., "Does the Perception that Stress Affects Health Matter? The Association with Health and Mortality," Health Psychology, September 2012, 31(5): pp. 677–684. A video of McGonigal's talk is available at https://www.ted.com/talks/kelly_mcgonigal_how_to_make_stress_your_friend

11   The guest's name was Dr. Gerald G. Jampolsky. See "Oprah On Forgiveness: This Definition Was 'Bigger Than An Aha Moment,'" Huffington Post, March 7, 2013.

12   Shawn Achor, The Happiness Advantage, p. 63.

13   "Jon Kabat-Zinn: Defining Mindfulness" at Mindful.org, retrieved February 26, 2017.

14   http://kk.org/thetechnium/1000-true-fans/

15   See Jane E. Dutton, *Energize Your Workplace: How to Create and Sustain High-Quality Connections at Work*, Jossey-Bass, 2003.

16   Dunn, Aknin, and Norton, "Spending Money on Others Promotes Happiness," Science, 319 (2008), pp. 1697–1688.

17   Phillippa Lally, Cornelia H. M. van Jaarsveld, Henry W. W. Potts, et al., "How Are Habits Formed: Modelling Habit Formation in the Real World," European Journal of Social Psychology, July 16, 2009

YOU'RE INVITED

The world is so empty if one thinks only of mountains, rivers & cities; but to know someone who thinks and feels with us, and who, though distant, is close to us in spirit, this makes the earth for us an inhabited garden.

— JOHANN WOLFGANG VON GOETHE

WE'VE CREATED A PLACE FOR YOU, THE MOMENT makers of the world, to connect, collaborate, create, and celebrate together. You are invited to join our online community, or as we say—our Front Row Family.

Visit FrontRowFactor.com/facebook and request to join a group of happy, creative, and generous people from around the world who choose to make the most of every moment by living life in the front row. I'll be there personally and I look forward to seeing you there.

If you haven't already done so, check out the free resources we created just for you at FrontRowFactor.com/experiment.

To connect with me on social media, you'll find me on Twitter and Instagram at @jonvroman and on Facebook at Facebook.com/jonvroman. Get access to the Front Row Factor podcast and all other resources at FrontRowFactor.com.

ACKNOWLEDGEMENTS

To you, the reader: Thank you for choosing to step up and be a moment maker for yourself and others. Thank you for the contributions you've already made, and will make, toward humanity. I love you.

To all our recipients and families who we've had the privilege of creating experiences for: You are the heart and soul of this book. Your courage inspires so many. The way you choose to live life in the front row has taught us all how to make the most of all the moments we have. Starting with our first ever front row experience and listed in order of date: Ethel Caroline "Effie" Huboky, Michael Anastasi, Ronni Cardenas, Amie Honza, Tom Anastasi, Kristin Devlin, Elizabeth "Beth" Todd, Glenna Kohl, Ralph "JR" Bucciarelli, Jr., Melinda Welsh, Peg Rosewitski, Ryan Coates, Tony Barron, Heather Savio, Sophie Darr, Franklin "Frank" Hall, Kevin Carpenter, Leona

Witherspoon, Michelle Rappaport, Suzzane FitzGerald, Tommy Grace, Ethan Williams, Mike Boyd, Andrew James Cherpak III, Elenora "Elly" Iadanza, Luke Ronco, Marisa Choate Johnson, Alan Henry, Jaiden Taylor, Phil Thomson, Lindsey Powell-Rensch, Jason Szumski, James Strong, Chris Mosier, Susie Henderson, Thomas Kay, Patricia Smith, Molly Kuhlenschmidt, Derrick Boykins, Louis "Poppy" Foresta, Dianna Boyer, Charlotte Langford, Abimael "Abi" Barrera, Mark Enders, Mike Leigh, Tanner Seebaum, Mia Gurevitz, Ryan Bendoff, Twan Hayes, Landon Marine, Kelsey Trusty-Bishop, Mandy Schneider, Rebecca Colon, Bridget Valko, Linda McKairnes, Wendy Hawkes, Robert Meyne, Cynea Valdes, Katherine Gamble, Kaitlyn Mazur, Geoff McLeod, Kadeen Alansari, Rachel Littman, Jack Burke, Mackenzie Cassidy, Kevin Walker, Dave Salzwedel, Kim Gilligan, Laura Rundle, Louis "Louie" Branson, Melissa (Powell) Weaver, Johanna Yemm Owen Frenia, Niki Quasney, Mike Chan, Tori Eccleston, Christopher "Chris" Stern, Grady Welch, Gina Moriarty, Chris Casey, Darren Prendergast, Nina Philipp, Ryan Biddle, Beth Hahn, Logan Johnson Lay, Ella Joy Won, Abbey Gunnell, Leigh Kirschner, Jan Poehlmann, Jackson Eddy, Jayden Avilla, Holly Gibbons, Darvece Monson, Cindy Cripps, Nicole Colasanti, and Ashley Pearce.

I love you all.

To my wife, Tatyana: Your spirit makes my heart sing. There's no person on earth I'd rather create front row moments with than you. You energize my soul and elevate every experience. Your passion for love and life only grows brighter with time. Thank you for supporting this book and every project I take on. You stand with me always. I choose you today, and every day. I'm forever your #1 fan. I love you.

To my boys, Tiger and Ocean: I love being your dad. You bring the deepest sense of meaning and purpose to my life. Your genuine love of life brings me endless joy. Keep following your heart, share your gifts and be conscious moment makers. Surround yourselves with people that bring out your best, and with those with whom you can share your best. I am very proud of you. I believe in you. I love you both.

To Mom and Dad: You gave me life. You showed me what true love and contribution looks and feels like. Thanks for creating so many front row moments for our family—these were the seeds for my life's work. The loving environment you provided and core values you demonstrated, have guided my life. Thank you for writing the very first check to Front Row Foundation in 2005. You've always been there—in the front row. I love you both.

To my sister, Kirsten: You're the best sister a brother could hope for. I love how our friendship continues to grow each and every year. Thank you for taking my calls at all hours of the day to chat about the book, read and re-read each chapter and for always cheering me on. You're smart, generous and kind. FRF is lucky to have you as our finance manager, along with stepping up wherever needed. I love you.

To my beautiful nieces, Payton and Kinsley: You are both kind, smart and loving girls. I'm honored to be in your front row and witness your magnificent lives. I cherish the front row moments we've created and look forward to the many epic adventures we'll have in the years ahead. I love you both.

To my mother-in-law, Tamara Kalinichenko: I'm so grateful that my boys have the opportunity to develop such a deep and loving relationship with their Babushka. You make countless sacrifices to improve the quality of life of everyone around you. Your thoughtfulness and giving spirit inspires me. Our family is unquestionably happier and healthier because of your selfless contributions and unending support. I love you.

To my Grandmother, Pauline Yoder: This December, as you celebrate 100 years of age, you're still living life in the front row! You are the ultimate moment maker. You bring love and light to every situation or person you encounter. You are a powerful force for good and my life is deeply enriched because of you. You've provided an example for the value of working hard, being adventurous and treating others with respect. I love you.

To my Aunts and Uncles: John & Patti Vroman; Jane Albert; Bob & Lana Yoder. And to the rest of my extended family Amie Stumbo, Chrystie Varn, The Frey Family (Rick, Joey, Jake, Amanda, Alexa and Jett), Mike Frey & Stacey Cabano, Dan & Lisa Vroman, Jennie Vroman & Brian Teitsworth, Kane

Yoder, Eileen Yoder, Jayson Yoder & Sue Castro, Anatoli & Olga Kalinichenko, and Rob & Veronica Yoder. I love you.

To my "Front Row" and brothers for life (in alphabetical order)

Andrew Smallwood: I hope my boys grow up to be just like you. You're smart and curious. You're kind and generous. Your leadership as the Chairman of the Board has been a game-changer for FRF. Many of my favorite conversations about life, business, and giving to the world have occurred in your company. You ask powerful questions, listen deeply, and offer incredible insight. I look forward to building with you in the years ahead. I love you.

Carey Smolensky: If I were to point to one person who truly lives life in the front row—it's you. You bring the "family feel" to FRF in such powerful way. Your steadfast service to our cause as a Board Member, fundraiser, event host, and ambassador has brought so much to the Front Row family. I'm deeply grateful for your friendship and know that our best moments in life are yet to come. Keep living with passion and helping others. I love you.

Hal Elrod: Your enthusiasm, courage and generosity inspire me. I've watched in admiration as you've stepped up time and time again in support of others. You've impacted my personal life and FRF in immeasurable ways. Your hosting Chris Mosier's Front Row experience, integrating the annual FRF celebration into BestYearEverLive.com and donating money from the sales of The Miracle Morning book series . . . and that's just scratching the surface. I can't wait for your UFC event—front row! I love you.

Jamie Baugher: We ran our first ultramarathon together, started a charity together, and shared some epic "firsts". You've consistently raised the bar and challenged the status quo, which has unquestionably made me a better person. You've been there to support me during my darkest hours and celebrated my big wins. I'm grateful for our friendship. I love you.

John Kane: You are the moment maker. The positive impact you've had on my life as well as within FRF is immeasurable and inexplicable. You've believed in me so much—I learned to believe in myself. You bring out my best. This book would not be possible without you. When my boys grow up, I hope they can experience a meaningful friendship built on trust, love, and countless front row moments—just like ours. Oh... and one more thing. You got a front row tattoo! I still can't believe it. I love you.

Jon Berghoff: So many of the best ideas with FRF can be traced back to your strategic design. You've believed in this mission from day one. You have given limitless time, energy, and resources to serve our recipients, their families, and the entire community. Together, we've had some epic adventures that are some of my most cherished memories. From your wedding celebration on top of Half Dome in Yosemite to running an ultramarathon through the night in Atlantic City—you never cease to elevate the experience of life so that everyone can flourish. I value and appreciate you. I love you.

John Ruhlin: You make magic happen. As I write this, I'm looking at the framed picture of Sophie that you gave me. Your gift-giving is legendary and has impacted my world and so many others. You not only wrote the book on gifting, you've lived out those principles for more than a decade within FRF. You've been behind the scenes, opening doors, donating time, talent, and treasure to make experiences possible and magical for countless recipients. I love you.

So many of the individuals I want to recognize have contributed as volunteers, staff, donors, vendors, board members, and in so many other ways. I may or may not have mentioned their names in all of the categories where they've made an impact. Some people would have been listed a dozen times. Additionally, if I've missed anyone along the way, my apologies.

I want you to know I love and appreciate you.

To the Front Row Team, past and present: Without each of you, none of this is possible. You've selflessly given your heart and soul to raise money, create experiences, build systems, and cultivate our incredible culture and community where everyone feels welcome and is supported in living life to the fullest. You're creative, hard-working, and loving. **Thank you to:** Alex Blake (Social Media), Andrew Smallwood (Communications and Development), Audrey Williams (Communications), Kaile Monroe (Event Director), Kellie Leeper (Event Director), Kirsten Vroman (Finance Manager), Mara Berghoff (Director), Mary Ann Reponte (Online support), Michelle Macirella (Support), Rebecca Herzog (Event Director), and Shannon Coon (Event Director). I love you all.

To those who gathered together when Front Row Foundation was just an idea and brought this to life: Al DiLeonardo, Alicia Anderer, Amy Apollo, Bernice Apollo, Betsy Crouch, Jamie Baugher, John Kane, Jon & Mara Berghoff, Loretta DiCiano, Ryan Snow, Shannon Connor, Sue Yerou, Tracy Kane and Trent Booth. I love you all.

To the Board of Directors past and present: Angie & Warren Macdougall, Andrew Ironmonger, Betsy Crouch, Carey Smolensky, Cody Hayes, Dave Powders, Drew Eckman, Earl Kelly, Jeff Bry, Jen Dulin, John Kane, John Ruhlin, Jon Berghoff, Katherine Otway, Michael Anastasi, and Mike Coscetta. I love you all.

To the Ambassador Team (Our monthly donors): You are the heartbeat of the charity. More than 150 rockstars contribute monthly—some for over a decade now. Although we don't list every name here, this team is led by people like Alicia Messa, Andrew Smallwood, The Burke Family, Carey & Diane Smolensky, Casey McCarthy, Chris Heigel, Christy Solar, Dana Malstaff, DJ & Jen Dulin, Geoff & Sally

Smallwood, Hal & Ursula Elrod, Heidi Murray, Jeff & Debbie Bry, Jeff Latham, Joe Perkins, John Lee Dumas, John & Christine Edwin, John & Monica Israel, John & Tracy Kane, John Roach, Jon & Mara Berghoff, Jon Rivas, Josh Painter, Josh & Amiee Mueller, Judi & Kevin Finneran, Julian Landry, Justin Grable, Kevin & Amy Smits, Lance & Brandy Salazar, Matt Aitchison, Matt & Priya Recore, Michael Anastasi, Michael Content, Michael Coscetta, Rick & Danna Vroman, Scot Lowry, Stephen & Jessica Putonti, Tara Hardern, Tim & Tina Rhode, Trey Ketcham, Victor & Lydia Ramirez. I love you all.

To the Front Row Fundraisers and Sponsors: This group is led by people like Axis Construction (Bill Bostic & Gary Williams), Cutco Foundation, Dove Chocolate Discoveries (Becca Teichman and John Wycoff), Cutco Closing Gifts (Tony Carlston), Janine Eidenberg, John Kane, Kaile Monroe, Kristen Waby, Maurices (Nancy Adams), Rowan University (Constantine Alexakos), The Rising Sun Division (Wes Frank), The Rocky Mountain Division (Drew Frank), The Influence Group (Michael Owens), The TKO Division (Dave Powders), Theresa Casey, Topfer Family Foundation, University of Dayton (Dr. Peter Titlebaum). I love you all.

To Financial Contributors: There are many who have given their treasures: This group is led by people like Adam & Melinda Stock, Alicia Messa, Amiee & Josh Mueller, Brianna Greenspan, Chuck Widger, Hal & Ursula Elrod, Heidi Murray, Jason Vanzin, Josh Painter, Mike & Lindsay McCarthy, Rick & Danna Vroman, Scot Lowry, Scott Groves,

Susan Rosengren, Sylvain LaPointe, and Sue Adams. I love you all.

To the many contractors, vendors, and friends who've provided a service, product, or gift to FRF: Angela Wolf Video, LLC (Angela Wolf), Brand Alliance (Gentry Harrington), Conedera Studios (Nick Conedera), CSP Worldwide (Carey Smolensky), Custom Specialty Promotions (Diane Smolensky), Cutco Cutlery, Dan Humparpzoomian (Graphic Design), Fathom Digital Marketing (Scot Lowry), Flourishing Leadership Institute (Jon Berghoff), John Halfmann Signs (John Halfmann and Margie Thompson), Live Nation, Luminaria Photography (Michelle Macirella), NGNG Enterprises (Amber Vilhauer), Seequs (Stephen Christopher and Andrea Sandidge), Valley Oak (Matthew Rzepka), Vitamix Corporation, . I love you all.

A special thanks to many others who've given in unique and special ways, either by creating introductions, offering counsel, securing tickets, sharing talent, generating funding, coordinating experiences, showing us how to live life in the front row or countless other ways you've stepped up: This group is led by people like Adam Jester, Bill Gooch, Brianna Greenspan, Carl Drew, Carolyn Bostrack, Charlie Connely, Chris Blum, Chris Otto, Courtney Mullins, Christy Solar, Darin Wolf, Eva Littman, Gail Goodwin, Helen Brown, Honoree Corder, Jason MacKenzie, Jeffrey Paul Bobrick, Jeff Bouwman, Jeremy "Brotha James" Reisig, Jeremiah Eskew, John Edwin, Kris Mailepors, Kristine Gick,

Kyle Smith, Laura MacMinn, Lori MacHenry, Melissa & Suzi Weaver, Mike Bankus, Mike Eaton, Mike Monroe, Monica McGuire, Nikki Hornsberry, Nina Perez, Patrick Barry, Randy Gilbert, Rob Brandt, Sally Smallwood, Sean Douglas, Sena Able, Sharinda Welton, Sherri Dickie, Simcha Gluck, Steve Hackman, Stuart Ferguson, Tiffany Swineheart and Tom Skawski. I love you all.

To those who've donated a percentage of your book sales to support FRF: This group is led by people like Carey Smolensky's Living Life with Passion and Helping Others, Hal Elrod's The Miracle Morning, Brianna Greenspan's The Miracle Morning Art of Affirmations, Jeff Bouwman's Your Income, Your Life, Justin Ledford's Visions to the Top, Melissa Weaver's Reconstruction - Defying Cancer and Building a More Purposeful Life, and Mike Merriam's Closer Than You Think. I love you all.

To everyone in our Front Row Family: For anyone we haven't listed and are directly or distantly connected, we appreciate and honor you. Thanks to all of our Front Row Dads. Thanks to those who've attended our annual summit where we learn to be moment makers while co-creating the future of FRF. Thanks to all those who've attended our annual celebration at Best Year Ever Blueprint. I love you all.

To The World's Greatest Book Team: Andrew Smallwood (Reading & Editing Team), Azul Terronez (Coaching), Bailey Reagan (Research), Bex Herzog (Reading Team), Brianna Greenspan (Reading Team), Christina

Culbertson (Formatting & Design), Emeka Ossai (Kindle Publishing), Hal Elrod (Foreword), Honorée Corder (Coaching), John Kane (Coaching), Jon Berghoff (Coaching), Julianna Raye (Reading Team), Justin Ledford (Launch support), Kellie Leeper (Writing Team), Kirsten Vroman (Writing Team), Lance Salazar (Reading Team), Leslie Watts (Editing), Leslie Staller (Reading Team), Natalie Janji (Reading Team), Nick Mayo (Design), Paul Joy (Reading Team), Ramon Rouse (Book Launch), Sarah Andrus (Writing), Tim Walker (Proofreading), Amber Ludwig-Vilhauer (Book Launch). I love you all.

To a few of my amazing friends, mentors, and teachers who've played an important role in a variety of ways (I should mention that those names shared throughout the entire acknowledgments section, I also consider friends, mentors, and teachers): Amy Port, Aviva Bennett Tribuch, Aysen Ulupinar, Ben Schemper, Bob Burg, Bobby Audley, Brad Weimert, Brad Johnson, Brendan Burchard, Brian Rocha, Bryan Harrell, David Brower, Derek Sivers, Donna Muriel, Ed Paul, Eli Shine, Gisselle Baugher, Isaac Tolpin, Jason Scheckner, Jayson Gaignard, Jeff Hoffman, Jeff Sawyer, Jim Sheils, John Lee Dumas, Jon Stewart, Jordan Harbinger, Josh Shipp, Justin Donald, Keith & Re'shon Townes, Larry Hagner, Mark Mills, Marly Doty, Mary Hattum, Matthew Kelly, Matt Duncan, Matt Recore, Matt Tenney, Michael Port, Michelle Burger, Nick Hemmert, Pat Dillon, Pat Petrini, Paulette Cazares, Phil Monk, Phoebe Mroczek, Robert Follis, Rudy Ruettiger, Ryan Rouse, Sharissa Sosa, Stan Pearson,

Stacey & Paul Martino, Stephen Scoggins, Tim Sims, Tim Rhode, Tim Ferriss, Tom Krieglstein, Tony Robbins, Tuan Nguyen, and Yanik Silver. I love you all.

My Vector Marketing and Cutco Family: Being part of this incredible company has changed my life. The culture is one that attracts, creates and supports many of the world's most incredibly talented, fun and generous people. I wouldn't be who I am today if not for my extraordinary Vector/Cutco family. To Rich Plaskon, At age 19, you changed my life by giving me an opportunity to be part of the Vector/Cutco family. To Jim Stitt Jr and Jim Stitt Sr, I'm forever grateful for your ongoing support. To the CSP Community, led by people like Aaron Ludin, Adam Sobieski, Alicia Anderer, Andy Jeanty, Carl & Heather Drew, Curtis Jacques, Dave Stewart, David Scoggins, Geri Azinger, Jeffrey Paul Bobrick, John Ruhlin, John Israel, Josh Mueller, Katie Heaney, Margo Myers-Policastro, Mike Lonzetta, Ray Ciafardini, Ray Reed, Sam Mickle and Tony Carlston. To the District and Division Manager team, led by people like Chris Hammond, Chris Heigel, Dave Powders, Drew Frank, Jason Heinritz, Jeff Gamboa, John Wasserman, Matt King, Nick Matlack, Ryan Trembler, Trey Ketcham, and Wes Frank. To the Regional Manager Team, Dan Casetta, Earl Kelly, Jeff Bry, Loyd Reagan, Mike Muriel, and Scott Dennis. To the Executive Team, led by people like Al DiLeonardo, Amar Dave, Bruce Goodman, Connor Boram, Dave Bush, Helen Brown, Jake Coon, John Kane, John Whelpley, Loretta DiCiano, Mallory O'Neil, Mike Lancellot, Mike Monroe, Nikki Divece, Scott Gorrell, Steve Pokrzyk, Stu Smith, Tim

McCreadie, and Trent Booth. To Cutco Canada, led by people like Angie Macdougall, Jim Kalil, Joe Cardillo, Mike McDonald and Shayla Dupont Wey. To the Sales Promotion managers, led by people like Joel Rioux, Kyle Smith and Travis Griffin. To the Regional Teams, led by people like Cindy Mohrman, Erin Long, Jay Perez, and Natasha Maldonado. To my Olean friends, led by people like Adam Jester, Chris Otto, Deb Zmed, Tami Yorke, and Trinette Brewer.

I love you all.

THE FRONT ROW POSE

Throughout the book, you've seen a few pictures of people putting their hands up and striking a "front row pose." The symbolism of pointing your fingers to the sky, arms in the shape of a "V" demonstrates the powerful emotions often felt during front row moments.

Within our community, whenever a picture is taken, someone will undoubtedly say "FRONT ROW!!!!" and the hands all go up.

Over the past 11 years, this has become an iconic pose for front row pictures—from recipients to donors and everyone in between.

We've had people send in pictures from more than 30 countries around the world, celebrating front row moments in their lives. We've seen front row pictures of people doing everything from scuba diving to skydiving—from running with the bulls to running marathons. We've even seen this pose come alive digitally, where you might see—\o/—as another way to communicate "congrats, awesome or way to go."

During your front row moment experiment, we invite you to join in, snap a few "hands up" pictures and share them with us in the Facebook group (FrontRowFactor.com/facebook) or on your favorite social media account using the hashtag #FrontRowMoment.

ABOUT THE AUTHOR

JON VROMAN is on a mission to show you how to live life in the front row through the transformative art of moment making. He is a social entrepreneur, committed husband and father of two boys, and ultramarathon runner.

He is also the proud founder of the Front Row Foundation, a charity established in 2005 that creates unforgettable moments for individuals who are braving life-threatening illnesses. The organization transforms the lives by empowering individuals to "live life in the front row"™ by providing recipients a front row experience at the live event of their dreams.

As an award-winning speaker, Jon has given more than 750 keynote presentations for over a decade for many companies, organizations, universities, and associations. His clients include Vitamix, Cutco Cutlery, Maurices, St. Thomas Health, Keller Williams Realty, and the U.S. Navy. Jon's refreshingly effective and modern motivational edge that genuinely connects with his audience as he ignites their enthusiasm and challenges their status quo.

Host of the popular Front Row Factor Podcast, Jon interviews thought leaders about their personal strategies to help you strengthen your mindset, relationships, and environment so you can excel in every area of life. Many say that Jon's "superpower" is his ability to connect be it one-to-one or with a group. He draws out the best of each and every individual.

Jon is a fierce community builder who hosts live events including: The Front Row Dads Retreat, the Speaker Trainer Experience, the Front Row Personal Transformation and Co-Creation Summit, and the Front Row Foundation Celebration.

Find out more about Jon at www.FrontRowFactor.com

REQUEST JON'S KEYNOTE PRESENTATION

"Jon Vroman delivered massively. Our audience was profoundly impacted by the power of his message."

—JOHN KANE, Director of Sales, Vector Marketing

As an award-winning speaker, Jon has given more than 750 keynote presentations over the past decade for many companies, organizations, universities, and associations. His clients include Vitamix, Cutco Cutlery, Maurices, St. Thomas Health, Keller Williams Realty, and the U.S. Navy. Jon brings a refreshingly effective and modern motivational edge that genuinely connects with his audience as he ignites their enthusiasm and challenges their status quo.

"Attendees are leaving inspired and energized. It was exactly what we needed."

—TRISTIN CASTEEL, Manager Graduate Medical Education, Saint Thomas Health

"Inspiring, empowering—a call to action."

—NANCY ADAMS, Field Motivation and Recognition Manager, Maurices

The Front Row Factor keynote is a message with clear action steps that inspires people to act with courage and find opportunities in every challenge. It's about maximizing each moment and fulfilling potential.

To request that Jon speak for your organization, visit FrontRowFactor.com or email info@frontrowglobal.com

The Front Row Dads Retreat (FrontRowDads.com): Where fathers come together to form a brotherhood, deepen their sense of purpose as fathers, and co-create optimal family strategies. This experience allows for open and effective conversation.

The Front Row Personal Transformation and Co-Creation Summit (FrontRowFactor.com/Summit): This is a unique gathering for anyone wanting to take living life in the front row to the next level while helping co-create the future of the Front Row Foundation.

The Speaker Trainer Experience (SpeakerTrainerExperience. com): This is a highly-charged multi-day bootcamp to help you create a high-impact, transformative speech and deliver it with confidence, poise, and power.

The Best Year Ever Blueprint & Front Row Foundation Celebration (FrontRowFactor.com/bye): This event is designed to be highly experiential so that each attendee can create their personal playbook for the year and discover the fuel needed to bring their most compelling future visions to life.